Architecting AI Software Systems

Crafting robust and scalable AI systems for modern software development

Richard D Avila

Imran Ahmad

‹packt›

Architecting AI Software Systems

Portfolio Director: Kunal Chaudhari
Relationship Lead: Denim Pinto
Project Manager: K. Loganathan
Content Engineer: Deepayan Bhattacharjee
Technical Editor: Irfa Ansari
Copy Editor: Safis Editing
Indexer: Rekha Nair
Proofreader: Deepayan Bhattacharjee
Production Designer: Alishon Falcon
Growth Lead: Mansi Shah

First published: October 2025

Production reference: 1300925

Published by Packt Publishing Ltd.
Grosvenor House
11 St Paul's Square
Birmingham
B3 1RB, UK.

ISBN 978-1-80461-597-3

www.packtpub.com

Dedicated to my parents

Mom, your love and support are the bedrock that I stand on. Dad, you were my first and most influential teacher on architecture. Fate took you from us – I can only imagine the conversations we would have had about what intelligence, software, and architecture are. Your presence was with me in writing this book.

– Richard D Avila

I dedicate this book to my beloved father, Inayatullah Khan. His wisdom, values, and unwavering support continue to inspire me every day.

– Imran Ahmad

Contributors

About the authors

Richard D Avila is a software and systems architect with over two decades of industry experience building complex software systems. He has architected and held leadership roles for building a wide array of software systems to include complex simulations, autonomy, and data analytic systems. He has published in referred journals and industry publications on command-and-control theory, assurance architectures, multi-agent modeling, and machine learning. He was the first expert instructor on data analytics at the University of Maryland, Baltimore County – Training Centers. Before working as a software and systems architect, he served in the US Navy as a submarine officer.

I would like to thank the Packt editors for their support and guidance, and their insights and recommendations. Special thanks to Deepayan, Loganathan, and Denim.

Imran Ahmad, Ph.D, is an accomplished author and data scientist, widely recognized for his best-selling book *50 Algorithms Every Programmer Should Know*. He currently lends his expertise to the **Advanced Analytics Solution Center** (**A2SC**) within the Canadian Federal Government, where he harnesses machine learning algorithms for mission-critical applications.

In his 2010 doctoral thesis, he introduced a linear programming-based algorithm tailored for optimal resource assignment in expansive cloud computing landscapes. Later, in 2017, Dr. Ahmad pioneered the development of a real-time analytics framework, StreamSensing. This tool has become the cornerstone of several of his research papers, leveraging it to process multimedia data within various machine learning paradigms.

Outside of his governmental role, Dr. Ahmad holds a visiting professorship at the University of Ottawa. He has also been recognized as an authorized instructor for both Google Cloud and Microsoft. Currently, he is writing a forthcoming book on AI agents, scheduled for publication next year, and is actively engaged in research on large-scale AI agents, exploring how these systems can transform real-world applications.

I'm deeply grateful to my wife, Naheed, my son, Omar, and my daughter, Anum, for their unwavering support. A special nod to my parents, notably my father, Inayatullah, for his relentless encouragement to continue learning. Further appreciation goes to Loganathan, Denim, and Deepayan from Packt for their invaluable contributions.

About the reviewers

Mohamed Osam Abouahmed is a principal architect and consultant providing a unique combination of technical and commercial expertise to resolve complex and business-critical issues through the design and delivery of innovative, technology-driven systems and solutions.

Mohamed specializes in network automation solutions and smart systems development and deployment.

Mohamed's hands-on experience, underpinned by his strong project management and academic background, which includes a PMP Certification, Master of Global Management, Master of Business Administration (International Business), Master of Science in Computer Networking, and BSc in Electronics Engineering, has helped him develop and deliver robust solutions for multiple carriers, service providers, enterprises, and Fortune 200 clients including (among others) AT&T, Cisco Systems, and AWS.

He is the author of *Building Your AI Agents Army: A Hands-On Guide to Building Intelligent Autonomous Systems with Open-Source Tools* (ISBN 979-8283388939) and *Machine Learning in Microservices: Productionizing microservices architecture for machine learning solutions* (ISBN: 978-1804612149).

Ajay Soni is the creator of the **Verb-Oriented Middleware Architecture (VOMA)** and the **Verb-Object Graph Architecture (VOGA)**, paradigms established to integrate governance, explainability, and auditable processes into complex AI workflows. With over two decades of experience as a systems architect, AI researcher, and software engineer, his work has impacted high-stakes domains including quantitative finance, aerospace and defense, and enterprise AI. A strong proponent of **Model-Based Systems Engineering (MBSE)**, Ajay uses SysML to bridge the gap between high-level architectural design and robust, practical implementation. His research focuses on enabling real-time, autonomous decision-making on resource-constrained edge devices, ensuring every action is both transparent and compliant.

Through his company, Enjector Software, Ajay has developed a comprehensive platform for trusted autonomy. His expertise has been honed in demanding environments, having architected real-time fraud detection platforms at Barclays, developed large-scale pricing and risk systems at BNP Paribas, and designed distributed, safety-critical software for the Tempest fighter jet program at Leonardo. This background informs his perspective as a reviewer, bringing a meticulous focus on how governance, explainability, and real-time performance are integrated into complex systems. This is his first contribution as a book reviewer.

I appreciate the opportunity to review this insightful book and thank the authors and publishing team. I am also grateful to my family, friends, and colleague Dr. Indu Bhalla for their support and for the valuable discussions that have shaped my perspective on autonomous systems. These conversations have reinforced the importance of ethical governance, which guides my evaluations and reflects the collaborative spirit of my work.

Table of Contents

Part II: Architecting AI Systems   73

Chapter 4: Conceptual Design for AI Systems   75

Chapter 6: Design, Integration, and Testing — 119

Chapter 8: Insights and Future Directions 165

Chapter 9: Unlock Your Book's Exclusive Benefits 173

Preface

The age of **Artificial Intelligence (AI)** is upon us. Every day, new applications, extensions, or improvements in almost all aspects of life are being impacted by AI technologies. These technologies are almost entirely realized in complex software.

Building complex software is a challenge that requires disciplined and methodical effort to engineer. Many times, when complex software systems fail, it is usually that the architecture of the system failed, rather than a specific algorithmic or implementation detail. There exist best practices and lessons learned for building complex software. There also exist plenty of references on the theory and implementation of AI technologies.

There do not exist many references for how to build complex software that has AI technologies at its heart.

The authors' main tenet is that the application of architecting concepts and practices is a key enabler to building complex AI software. In the pages that follow, we will discuss what some of the challenges facing the builder of a complex AI system are. You will learn how you can adapt and use the lessons from architecting to structure and guide the development of a software system.

The book looks to balance theory and application: theory so that recommendations are grounded and can be understood, and application so that the book can be useful to you in the here and now. This book is the culmination of decades of experience of the authors with hard-earned lessons, both positive and negative. The age of AI is here; we hope this book will be another tool in your toolbox.

Who this book is for

There are three main audiences for this book:

1. A software architect or engineering manager who wants to expand their knowledge of how to build a complex AI-centric software system. The book gives a combination of theory and practical insights. The guidance in the book can be readily used to structure project gates and team tasking.

2. This book can be helpful to a technology executive, chief technology officer, or vice president of engineering. The book gives insight to aid in understanding the activities present in a major systems development. The executive can also gain visibility into key risks in system development. By knowing how to build AI-enabled systems, the executive can positively influence how the organization's strategy can be infused into the final systems.

3. This book can be used by an aspiring AI architect to learn the domain. This book will give insight into the major themes of architecting, provide references, and identify what areas can be focused on for further professional development.

What this book covers

Chapter 1, Fundamentals of AI System Architecture, provides an overview of the challenges and opportunities for building AI systems.

Chapter 2, The Case for Architecture, gives a short overview of architecture as a discipline and how architects have created and adapted tools to build complex structures.

Chapter 3, Software Engineering and Architecture, discusses how architecture concepts impact software engineering and can be used to improve the engineering of complex software.

Chapter 4, Conceptual Design for AI Systems, discusses one of the most important phases that the architect leads, the tools used, and the artifacts created to deliver a strong conceptual design.

Chapter 5, Requirements and Architecture for AI Pipeline, delves into the first aspects of post-conceptual design activities and lays a conceptual foundation for building an AI pipeline.

Chapter 6, Design, Integration, and Testing, gives a robust walk-through of design steps, the use of software tactics and patterns, and considerations for how an architecture impacts testing.

Chapter 7, Architecting a Generative AI System – A Case Study, provides a case study of how an AI system can be engineered for a help desk support system.

Chapter 8, Insights and Future Directions, concludes the content of the book and summarizes key points that we would want you to remember most.

Download the color images

We also provide a PDF file that has color images of the screenshots/diagrams used in this book. You can download it here: `https://packt.link/gbp/9781804615973`

Conventions used

There are a number of text conventions used throughout this book.

Bold: Indicates a new term, an important word, or words that you see on the screen. For instance, words in menus or dialog boxes appear in the text like this. For example: "Select **System info** from the **Administration** panel."

Warnings or important notes appear like this.

Tips and tricks appear like this.

Get in touch

Feedback from our readers is always welcome.

General feedback: If you have questions about any aspect of this book or have any general feedback, please email us at `customercare@packt.com` and mention the book's title in the subject of your message.

Errata: Although we have taken every care to ensure the accuracy of our content, mistakes do happen. If you have found a mistake in this book, we would be grateful if you reported this to us. Please visit `http://www.packt.com/submit-errata`, click **Submit Errata**, and fill in the form.

Piracy: If you come across any illegal copies of our works in any form on the internet, we would be grateful if you would provide us with the location address or website name. Please contact us at `copyright@packt.com` with a link to the material.

If you are interested in becoming an author: If there is a topic that you have expertise in and you are interested in either writing or contributing to a book, please visit `http://authors.packt.com/`.

Share your thoughts

Once you've read *Architecting AI Software Systems*, we'd love to hear your thoughts! Scan the QR code below to go straight to the Amazon review page for this book and share your feedback.

https://packt.link/r/1804615978

Your review is important to us and the tech community and will help us make sure we're delivering excellent quality content.

Part 1

Architecting Fundamentals

In *Part 1* of the book, an overview is given of how architecture concepts impact software systems. This part walks you through the principle considerations in *Chapter 1*. Then, a short synopsis of architecting is described in *Chapter 2*. Finally, in *Chapter 3*, we discuss the impact architecting has on software engineering.

The following chapters are included in this part:

- *Chapter 1, Fundamentals of AI System Architecture*
- *Chapter 2, The Case for Architecture*
- *Chapter 3, Software Engineering and Architecture*

1

Fundamentals of AI System Architecture

The recent surge of public interest in **Artificial Intelligence (AI)**, particularly with the rise of generative AI, has ignited a wave of excitement and demand for comprehensive AI solutions. This heightened interest extends beyond tech enthusiasts and researchers to businesses, governments, and individuals seeking to harness AI's power to solve real-world problems and enhance their capabilities. In this landscape, the architecture of AI systems, which defines their structure, components, and interactions, plays a pivotal role in shaping the development and deployment of effective AI solutions.

AI has emerged as a transformative force, revolutionizing industries and reshaping the way we interact with technology and the world around us. At its core, AI refers to computational models that mimic human cognitive functions, including learning from data, recognizing patterns, making decisions, and even interacting with their environment. This revolutionary technology spans a wide spectrum, from simple rule-based systems to sophisticated deep learning models, each with unique applications and capabilities.

A major aspect of any AI system is that the results of the inference being done need to be relevant and trusted. To ensure trust is gained and maintained, the use of strong architecture is paramount. One not only architects the technology but also how the technology is going to be used, managed, and evaluated by the span of stakeholders. The stakeholders need to be able to pinpoint issues, rapidly correct model parameters, and deploy changes in a deliberate and rapid manner. In more common parlance, the architecting and supporting processes can be described as "guard rails." How one employs guard rails is very specific to the domain and use case that is to use the AI technology. There are classes of guard rails that can be discussed – for example, the use of canaries to judge model correctness from a known gold standard, time and data flow metrics to judge model performance, and the use of filters and robust data quality checks so that only consistent and correct data enters the system. Another class of guardrails is human system interfaces, such as alerting frameworks to classify errors and monitors, the use of troubleshooting tools, and preset protocols for handling unexpected errors. Written procedures or guidance from modeling allow for the maintenance of a system without the need to call upon the model developer to do troubleshooting.

Trust is a paramount consideration for system success, so one needs to architect a system with that in mind. In many ways, the presentation and lessons learned described in this book look to ensure trust in an AI system.

This chapter highlights, in a broad sense, the key aspects of AI architecture considerations that drive a successful AI implementation. The topics are as follows:

- Introduction and key AI concepts
- Components of an AI system
- AI technologies and microservices
- AI systems and technical considerations
- Deployment considerations

Getting the most out of this book — get to know your free benefits

Unlock exclusive **free** benefits that come with your purchase, thoughtfully crafted to supercharge your learning journey and help you learn without limits.

Here's a quick overview of what you get with this book:

Next-gen reader

Our web-based reader, designed to help you learn effectively, comes with the following features:

- ⟲ **Multi-device progress sync:** Learn from any device with seamless progress sync.
- 📖 **Highlighting and notetaking:** Turn your reading into lasting knowledge.
- 🔖 **Bookmarking:** Revisit your most important learnings anytime.
- ☀ **Dark mode:** Focus with minimal eye strain by switching to dark or sepia mode.

Figure 1.1: Illustration of the next-gen Packt Reader's features

Interactive AI assistant (beta)

Our interactive AI assistant has been trained on the content of this book, to maximize your learning experience. It comes with the following features:

❖ Summarize it: Summarize key sections or an entire chapter.

❖ AI code explainers: In the next-gen Packt Reader, click the Explain button above each code block for AI-powered code explanations.

Note: The AI assistant is part of next-gen Packt Reader and is still in beta.

Figure 1.2: Illustration of Packt's AI assistant

DRM-free PDF or ePub version

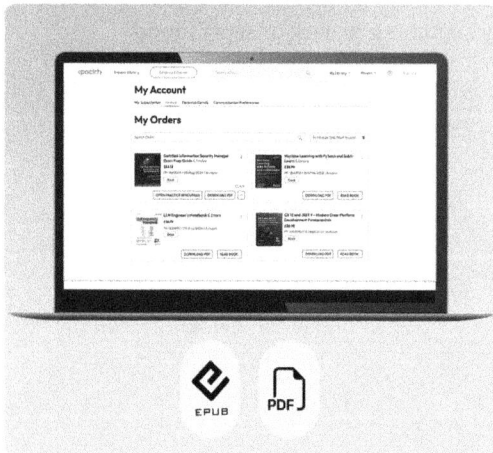

Learn without limits with the following perks included with your purchase:

⊞ Learn from anywhere with a DRM-free PDF copy of this book.

⊟ Use your favorite e-reader to learn using a DRM-free ePub version of this book.

Figure 1.3: Free PDF and ePub

Unlock this book's exclusive benefits now UNLOCK NOW

Scan this QR code or go to `https://packtpub.com/unlock`,
then search for this book by name. Ensure it's the correct
edition.

Note: Keep your purchase invoice ready before you start.

Introduction to AI systems: architecting the future of intelligence

AI systems are the embodiment of AI, acting as the engines that power intelligent applications
and services. These systems are intricate constructs, meticulously designed to perform a diverse
range of tasks, from image recognition and natural language processing to autonomous decision-
making and complex problem-solving.

The architecture of an AI system functions as a detailed technical blueprint, specifying its structural
organization and the precise interactions between its various components. These components
include the following:

- **Hardware infrastructure**: CPUs for general processing, GPUs for parallel computation,
  TPUs for tensor operations, and specialized AI accelerators
- **Software frameworks**: TensorFlow, PyTorch, JAX, and other libraries that enable model
  development
- **Algorithmic implementations**: Machine learning algorithms, neural network architectures,
  and inference engines
- **Data pipelines**: ETL processes, feature stores, and data management systems

All these elements work in a coordinated operation to enable the system to fulfill its designed
objectives efficiently and reliably.

A well-architected AI system achieves several critical technical requirements:

- **Optimal performance**: Maximizes computational efficiency to deliver responsive and accurate results with minimal latency. This involves an optimized model design, efficient resource allocation, and hardware-aware implementations that fully utilize available computing capabilities.

- **Scalability**: Handles growing workloads and expanding datasets through both horizontal scaling (adding more machines) and vertical scaling (adding more powerful machines) without performance degradation. Modern AI architectures must accommodate increasing data volumes, user bases, and computational demands.

- **Efficiency**: Reduces computational resource consumption, energy usage, and operational costs through techniques such as model quantization, knowledge distillation, and optimized inference paths. Efficient AI systems minimize their resource footprint while maintaining functional effectiveness.

- **Reliability**: Ensures consistent operation with high-availability metrics, even when facing unexpected data patterns, input variations, or system failures. This requires robust error handling, graceful degradation capabilities, and comprehensive monitoring systems. Given that AI technologies can be both deterministic and non-deterministic, consideration must be given to allow for human intervention. This intervention needs to span the gamut from simple monitoring to a full suite of testing infrastructure.

- **Security**: Implements comprehensive data protection measures and defends against adversarial attacks, data poisoning, and model vulnerabilities. AI systems must maintain data confidentiality and integrity, and be resilient against both traditional cybersecurity threats and AI-specific attacks.

- **Explainability**: Provides transparent visibility into algorithmic decision processes, supporting regulatory compliance, user trust, and system debugging. Modern AI architectures must balance performance with interpretability to meet growing demands for AI transparency.

The field of AI is constantly evolving, with new architectures and technologies emerging at a rapid pace. As we delve deeper into this fascinating domain, we will explore the various types of AI systems, their underlying principles, and the diverse applications that are shaping the future of technology and society.

What is an AI system?

An AI system is a computational model or a collection of models designed to perform tasks that typically require human intelligence. These systems are powered by algorithms and data, enabling them to learn from experience, adapt to new information, and make decisions or predictions.

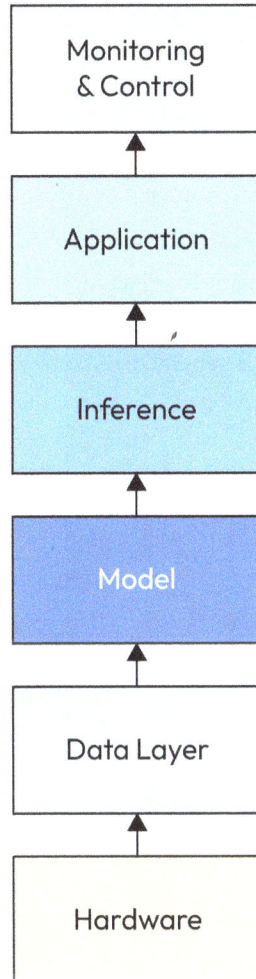

Figure 1.4: AI technology stack

From an implementation perspective, AI systems typically consist of several key layers:

1. **Hardware:** Encompasses compute resources such as CPU, GPU, TPUs, full-spectrum storage, and networking

2. **Data layer:** Handles data ingestion, storage, preprocessing, and feature engineering

3. **Model layer**: Contains the trained machine learning or deep learning models

4. **Inference layer**: Manages the execution of models against new data inputs

5. **Application layer**: Integrates AI capabilities into user-facing applications

6. **Monitoring layer**: Tracks system performance, data drift, and model health

AI systems can be classified into two broad categories:

- **Narrow AI (weak AI)**: These systems are designed to excel at specific tasks within a limited domain. Examples include image recognition software, spam filters, and recommendation engines. While they may be highly proficient at their designated tasks, they lack the ability to generalize their knowledge in other areas.

- **General AI (strong AI)**: This is a theoretical concept of an AI system that possesses human-level intelligence and can perform any intellectual task that a human can. It would have the ability to reason, plan, solve problems, learn from experience, and understand complex ideas across diverse domains. While general AI remains a distant goal, significant progress has been made in developing systems with increasingly sophisticated capabilities.

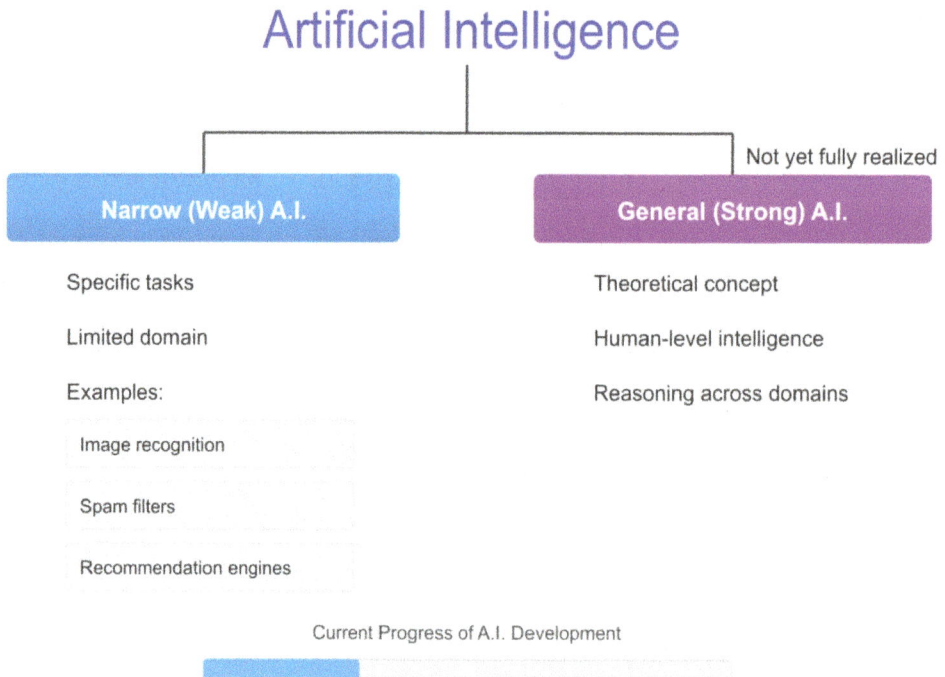

Figure 1.5: Classification of AI systems

🔍**Quick tip**: Need to see a high-resolution version of this image? Open this book in the next-gen Packt Reader or view it in the PDF/ePub copy.

📖**The next-gen Packt Reader** and a **free PDF/ePub copy** of this book are included with your purchase. Scan the QR code OR visit `https://packtpub.com/unlock`, then use the search bar to find this book by name. Double-check the edition shown to make sure you get the right one.

The pervasive impact of AI infrastructure: powering intelligent solutions across industries

Well-architected AI infrastructure, encompassing the hardware, software, and networks that support AI applications, is the driving force behind the transformative impact of AI across industries. This infrastructure enables the deployment and scaling of AI models, algorithms, and frameworks, unlocking their full potential to address complex challenges and deliver innovative solutions.

- Healthcare:
  - **Accelerated medical image analysis**: High-performance computing clusters and specialized hardware accelerators enable rapid processing of medical images, facilitating faster and more accurate diagnosis.
  - **Data-driven insights**: Scalable storage and processing infrastructure empowers AI-driven analytics on vast patient datasets, leading to personalized treatment plans and improved patient outcomes.
  - **Real-time monitoring**: Cloud-based AI infrastructure enables continuous monitoring of patient vitals and other health data, facilitating timely interventions and proactive care.

- **Finance:**

  - **Robust fraud detection:** Distributed computing and real-time analytics platforms empower AI models to detect fraudulent transactions with greater accuracy and speed, protecting financial institutions and consumers.

  - **Optimized trading strategies**: High-frequency trading algorithms leverage low-latency networks and powerful computational resources to execute trades with precision and efficiency, maximizing returns.

  - **Personalized financial services:** Cloud-based AI infrastructure enables the deployment of robo-advisors and other AI-powered tools that provide tailored financial advice and services to individuals.

- **Autonomous vehicles:**

  - **Real-time sensor fusion:** High-throughput data pipelines and edge computing infrastructure enable the rapid processing of sensor data from cameras, lidar, radar, and other sources, ensuring timely decision-making for autonomous vehicles.

  - **Enhanced object recognition:** Deep learning models trained on massive datasets and deployed on specialized hardware accelerators enable accurate and reliable identification of objects in the environment.

  - **Optimized navigation:** Cloud-based mapping and navigation services, combined with onboard AI processing, provide autonomous vehicles with real-time information and guidance for safe and efficient navigation.

The continued development and optimization of AI infrastructure will play a crucial role in realizing the full potential of AI across industries. By providing the foundation for performant and scalable AI solutions, this infrastructure is poised to transform the way we live and work.

Key components of AI system architectures

AI systems, in their essence, are complex structures designed to emulate human cognitive abilities such as learning, reasoning, and problem-solving. To achieve these capabilities, AI systems rely on a well-defined architecture comprising several interconnected components, each playing a crucial role in the overall functioning of the system. Understanding these key components is fundamental to comprehending the inner workings and potential of AI.

- **Data components:** Data serves as the lifeblood of any AI system, acting as the raw material upon which the system learns and improves. Data can exist in multiple forms:

  - **Structured data:** Organized in predefined formats such as databases and spreadsheets

  - **Semi-structured data:** Partially organized information such as JSON or XML files

  - **Unstructured data:** Raw information, including text documents, images, audio recordings, and video files

The quality, quantity, and relevance of the data significantly impact the AI system's performance and ability to generalize to new situations.

- **Algorithmic frameworks:** Algorithms are engines driving AI systems, providing instructions and logic for processing data and generating intelligent outputs. Machine learning algorithms, a subset of AI algorithms, empower systems to learn patterns and relationships from data, enabling them to make predictions, classifications, or decisions. Common algorithmic approaches in production AI systems include the following:

  - **Traditional machine learning:** Linear regression, random forests, gradient boosting, and support vector machines

  - **Deep learning: Convolutional neural networks (CNNs), Recurrent Neural Networks (RNNs),** transformers, and graph neural networks

  - **Reinforcement learning:** Q-learning, policy gradient methods, and actor-critic architectures

The selection of appropriate algorithms depends on the specific problem domain, available data characteristics, and performance requirements.

- **Model architectures:** Models represent the culmination of the learning process in AI systems. They are mathematical representations of the knowledge extracted from data, encapsulating the patterns, relationships, and insights discovered by the algorithms. These models can be simple or complex, depending on the nature of the task and the algorithm used. Model architectures range between the following:

  - **Simple linear models:** Easily interpretable but limited in capability

  - **Ensemble models:** Combining multiple simpler models for improved performance

  - **Deep neural networks:** Complex architectures with millions or billions of parameters

Once trained, models are used to make predictions or decisions on new, unseen data.

- **Infrastructure:** The infrastructure component encompasses the hardware and software resources that provide the computational power and environment necessary for AI systems to operate. Key infrastructure elements include the following:

    - **Computational resources**: High-performance servers, specialized AI accelerators (GPUs, TPUs, FPGAs), and distributed computing clusters
    - **Storage systems**: High-throughput, scalable storage for training data and model artifacts
    - **Networking components**: Low-latency interconnects for distributed training and inference

- **Development frameworks**: Software libraries such as TensorFlow, PyTorch, and Hugging Face that streamline AI development and deployment.

Understanding these key components and their interactions provides a solid foundation for comprehending the complex landscape of AI system architectures. By carefully designing and optimizing each component, researchers and engineers can build AI systems that are capable of tackling a wide range of tasks and applications, from image recognition and natural language processing to autonomous driving and drug discovery. The integration of AI capabilities into existing software stacks requires thoughtful architectural considerations to successfully incorporate intelligence while addressing the unique requirements that AI components introduce. These specific requirements and architectural approaches form the central focus of this book. Due to the complexity of AI systems, the nature of the deployment approach is paramount. The next section will discuss the use of microservice architectures that provide a balance between performance and modularity.

Microservice architectures: a modular approach to building complex AI systems

As **AI** systems grow in complexity, traditional monolithic architectures can become unwieldy, hindering development speed and flexibility. Microservice architectures offer a compelling alternative by breaking down these complex systems into smaller, independent services. Each microservice focuses on a specific function and communicates with others through well-defined APIs.

Advantages of microservices for AI

- **Enhanced agility and flexibility**: Teams can independently develop, deploy, and update each microservice, using the most suitable technologies and programming languages for each task. This accelerates development cycles and allows for easier experimentation and innovation.

- **Improved scalability**: Microservices can be scaled horizontally to meet specific demand, ensuring optimal resource utilization. For example, a service handling image processing can be scaled independently of a service responsible for natural language understanding.

- **Increased resilience and fault isolation**: If a microservice fails, the impact is localized, minimizing disruption to the entire system. This enhances overall reliability and simplifies troubleshooting.

- **Technological diversity**: Microservice architectures empower teams to leverage the best tools for each task, promoting innovation and allowing for gradual technology upgrades.

Challenges of microservice architectures

- **Increased complexity**: Managing a multitude of services and their interactions requires robust orchestration and monitoring tools. Service discovery, load balancing, and failure handling become critical considerations.

- **Communication overhead**: Excessive inter-service communication can introduce latency and impact overall performance. The careful design of APIs and communication patterns is essential to mitigate this issue.

- **Data consistency**: Maintaining data consistency across distributed services can be challenging. Strategies such as eventual consistency or distributed transactions may be required to ensure data integrity.

Real-world example: conversational AI microservices implementation

To illustrate how a microservices approach can streamline a conversational AI solution, let us examine a practical example that demonstrates how these principles come to life. This section explores a conversational AI system – such as a chatbot or virtual assistant – built using a four-service microservices architecture with an API gateway.

The four core microservices

Figure 1.6 illustrates the high-level design of our conversational AI system:

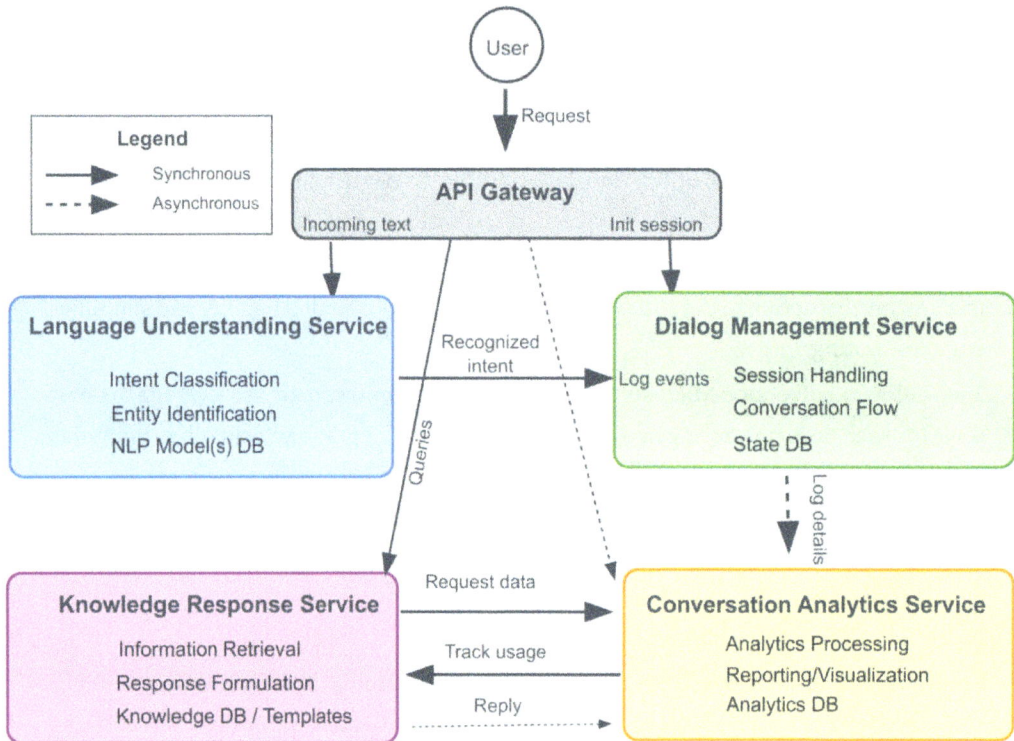

Figure 1.6: Conversational AI microservices

The architecture consists of four core specialized services plus an API gateway:

1. Language understanding service:

    - **Primary functions**: Intent classification, entity identification/extraction, and hosting of NLP models.

    - **Data and models**: References one or more NLP model databases (for example, transformer-based classifiers).

    - **Key interactions**: Receives the user's text (through the API gateway), determines the user's intent (e.g., "Check account balance"), and extracts relevant entities (e.g., "date," "location," "product name").

2. Dialog management service:

    - **Primary functions**: Oversees conversation flow, handles session state, and orchestrates the next step in the dialog.

    - **Data and state**: Maintains conversation context in a dedicated state database.

    - **Key interactions**: Logs conversation events (asynchronously) and updates or retrieves session details to guide the flow (e.g., "Greeting," "Confirmation," "Next step").

3. Knowledge response service

    - **Primary functions**: Retrieves relevant information and formulates responses. This might involve querying a knowledge base (e.g., FAQs, product info) or assembling template-based replies.

    - **Data and templates**: Stores domain-specific data in a knowledge DB and uses templates or generative mechanisms for response creation.

    - **Key interactions**: Receives queries from the dialog management service, finds or composes the best response, and returns it for final delivery to the user.

4. Conversation analytics service:

    - **Primary functions**: Processes logs and usage metrics for reporting, visualization, and deeper analytics (e.g., intent distribution, user satisfaction trends).

    - **Data and reporting**: Maintains analytics data in a separate database for dashboards or offline processing.

    - **Key interactions**: Collects asynchronous event logs from the dialog management service and other components to measure performance, track user behavior, and provide insights that could improve the system over time.

Role of the API gateway

Although not counted as one of the four microservices, the **API gateway** is a vital component at the front of the architecture. It does the following:

- Receives requests from the user (via text or other channels)
- Initializes the session and routes incoming data to the language understanding service
- Forwards recognized intents and updates to the dialog management service
- Passes replies from downstream services back to the user

By centralizing traffic management, the API gateway enforces consistent security, throttling, and monitoring policies while keeping each microservice isolated and independently scalable.

Conversation flow sequence

To illustrate how these microservices interact during a typical user journey, *Figure 1.7* shows the sequence of calls between them in a single conversation cycle:

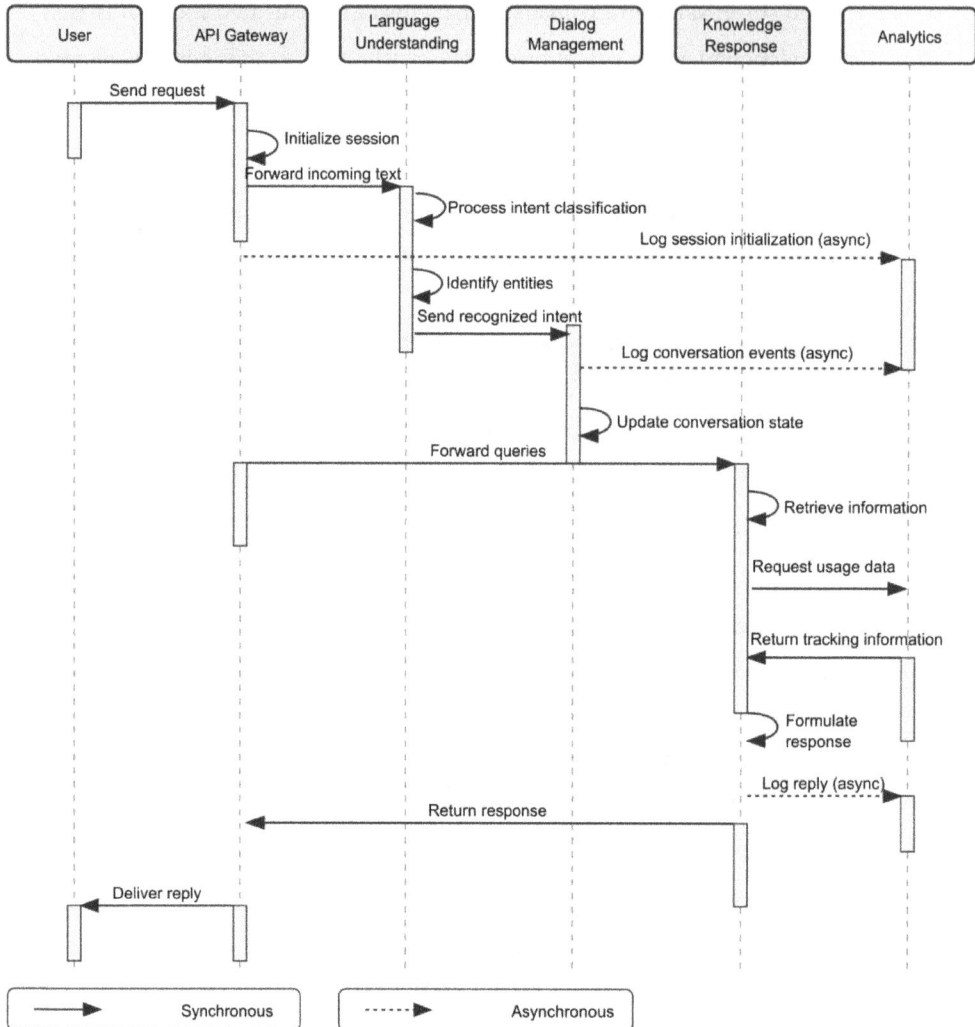

Figure 1.7: Sequence diagram between system components

The sequence progresses as follows:

1. **User → API gateway:** The user sends a request (e.g., a chat message). The API gateway initializes the session (if needed) and forwards the message to the language understanding service.

2. **Language understanding service**:

- Performs intent classification and entity identification.

- Returns a recognized intent (e.g., "CheckWeather") and any extracted entities (e.g., date, location) to the API gateway.

3. **Dialog management service**:

- Receives recognized intent from the API gateway.

- Logs conversation events (asynchronously) into the conversation analytics service.

- Updates or retrieves the **session state** (e.g., user's location or recent conversation context).

4. **Knowledge response service**:

- Once the dialog management service determines additional data is needed (e.g., weather info, product detail), it sends a **query** to the knowledge response service.

- This service fetches the necessary information or constructs a response template (e.g., "The weather for your location is sunny with 75°F...").

5. **Conversation analytics service (asynchronous logging)**:

- Continuously receives usage data and conversation logs from the dialog management service (and possibly from the knowledge response service).

- Processes and stores these logs for future reporting (e.g., monthly usage dashboards, model performance metrics).

6. **Reply to the user**:

- The knowledge response service's formulated answer is routed back through the dialog management service (if necessary, for final session updates) and then returned via the API gateway.

- The user receives the **reply** and the interaction concludes.

Key aspects of microservice communication

- Synchronous versus asynchronous calls:

  - Requests that must return immediately (e.g., generating a response for the user) use synchronous calls.

  - Logging or analytics operations are typically performed asynchronously to avoid slowing down the core conversation loop.

- Stateful versus stateless components:

    - Dialog management requires tracking session state, while other services (e.g., language understanding) often benefit from stateless designs for simpler scaling.

    - The dialog management service may require robust state management solutions, such as distributed caches or databases.

- Service autonomy:

    - Each microservice can be updated or replaced independently without affecting the rest of the system.

    - The language understanding service's NLP models may need frequent retraining. Because it is a separate service, such updates can be deployed without disrupting the other services.

- Data isolation:

    - Services manage their own domain data. Dialog management stores conversation state, knowledge response holds domain facts, and analytics maintains interaction logs.

    - Sensitive user data should be restricted to the dialog management service's state store when necessary, minimizing the exposure across the entire system.

Implementation considerations for conversational AI microservices

1. Scaling independently:

    - The language understanding service can be scaled up or down based on incoming message load (e.g., horizontal autoscaling for peak chat traffic).

    - The dialog management service maintains conversation state and may require different scaling strategies.

    - The knowledge response service often scales according to the complexity of information retrieval.

    - The conversation analytics service can be scaled separately, especially if analytics workloads (such as report generation) spike at different times than user requests.

2. Latency management:

    - Conversational AI systems aim for near real-time interactions. Minimizing network hops and communication overhead between services is crucial. Using lightweight communication protocols helps ensure the system performs well at scale.

3. Fault isolation:

- If one service fails (for instance, the knowledge response service goes offline), the rest of the system can still handle other tasks or offer fallback behaviors (e.g., an apology response or a redirect to a human agent).

4. Monitoring and observability:

- Robust logging and observability practices are crucial to ensure the system remains resilient to service failures or slowdowns. The conversation analytics service plays a key role in tracking system health and performance.

Why microservices for conversational AI?

Breaking down a conversational AI system into these four specialized services confers significant benefits in **maintainability**, **scalability**, and **team agility**. Each service can evolve independently, allowing rapid iteration on NLP models, conversation flows, and knowledge retrieval strategies without risking a "big bang" failure across the entire application.

At the same time, careful attention to **inter-service communication** is crucial. As the sequence diagram shows, multiple hops occur for every user request. Using lightweight communication protocols and distinguishing between synchronous and asynchronous operations helps maintain system responsiveness.

The example of conversational AI powerfully illustrates how the microservices approach enables balancing flexibility, fault tolerance, and iterative innovation. The lessons learned here – such as independently scaling critical services, isolating data for security, and ensuring graceful failure modes – apply broadly to a wide array of AI-driven solutions.

This real-world implementation pattern demonstrates that while microservices add complexity, the benefits they bring to AI systems – particularly those requiring frequent updates, variable scaling, and component-level innovation – often outweigh the challenges when properly architected and implemented.

Considerations for an AI system

Creating a well-designed AI system architecture necessitates careful consideration of several key factors. These factors ensure that the system not only functions effectively but also adapts to future demands and challenges.

Scalability: handling growing data and model complexity

AI systems often encounter growing volumes of data and increasingly complex models. Scalability is the ability of a system to handle this growth without compromising performance. Effective strategies include the following:

- **Horizontal scaling**: This involves adding more compute resources to distribute the workload. For instance, in a cloud environment, you might deploy additional virtual machines or containers to handle increased traffic. Kubernetes can orchestrate these containers, ensuring that the workload is evenly distributed.

- **Vertical scaling**: Enhancing existing resources with more powerful hardware. For example, upgrading a server's CPU or GPUs, adding more RAM, or using SSDs instead of HDDs to improve I/O performance.

- **Distributed computing**: Utilizing frameworks such as Apache Spark or Hadoop to process data across multiple nodes. This approach breaks down large datasets into smaller chunks that can be processed in parallel, significantly reducing processing time. For instance, Spark's **Resilient Distributed Datasets** (**RDD**s) allow for in-memory processing, which is much faster than traditional disk-based processing.

Performance: optimization techniques

In many AI applications, real-time or near-real-time processing is crucial. Techniques to optimize performance include the following:

- **Hardware acceleration**: Leveraging GPUs or TPUs for computationally intensive tasks – for example, TensorFlow and PyTorch can utilize CUDA cores in NVIDIA GPUs to accelerate deep learning model training.

- **Parallel processing**: Dividing tasks into smaller sub-tasks that can be executed concurrently. In Python, libraries such as multiprocessing or concurrent.futures can be used to parallelize tasks – for instance, training multiple models simultaneously or processing different data batches in parallel.

- **Algorithm optimization**: Choosing or designing algorithms with lower computational complexity. For example, using approximate nearest neighbor algorithms for large-scale similarity search instead of exact methods, which are computationally expensive.

Reliability: fault tolerance, error handling, and redundancy

Reliability is paramount, especially in critical applications. To ensure system uptime and data integrity, strategies such as fault tolerance, error handling, and redundancy are employed:

- **Fault tolerance**: The system can continue operating even if some components fail. For example, in a microservices architecture, if one service fails, others can continue to function. Tools such as Netflix's Hystrix can be used to implement circuit breakers to manage failures.

- **Error handling**: Mechanisms are in place to detect and correct errors gracefully – for instance, using try-catch blocks in code to handle exceptions and logging errors for further analysis.

- **Redundancy**: Critical components are duplicated to prevent single points of failure – for example, using RAID configurations for disk storage or deploying services in multiple availability zones in cloud environments to ensure high availability.

Security: data privacy and model robustness

AI systems often handle sensitive data, making security a top priority. Key considerations include the following:

- **Data encryption**: Protecting data at rest and in transit – for instance, using AES encryption for data stored in databases and TLS for data transmitted over networks. The use of encryption approaches needs to be considered and tested thoroughly to scope the impact on model and system performance.

- **Access control**: Implementing strict authorization and authentication mechanisms – for example, using OAuth 2.0 for secure API access and **role-based access control** (**RBAC**) to manage permissions.

- **Model robustness**: Guarding against adversarial attacks that could manipulate the system. Techniques such as adversarial training, where the model is trained on both normal and adversarial examples, can help improve robustness. Additionally, you can deploy anomaly detection systems to monitor for unusual patterns in data input.

Data modeling: catalogs and ontologies

In the realm of AI, data is not just a valuable asset but the very foundation upon which intelligent systems are built. As AI models rely heavily on vast amounts of data to learn and make informed decisions, effective management and organization of this data becomes paramount. This is where data catalogs and ontologies step in as indispensable tools for navigating the complexities of data landscapes within AI architectures.

Catalogs serve as centralized repositories of metadata, providing comprehensive information about the data assets within an AI system. They act as a comprehensive index, offering insights into the data's location, schema, lineage, quality, and other relevant attributes. By consolidating this information in a structured and accessible manner, data catalogs empower data scientists, engineers, and analysts to gain a deeper understanding of their data resources, streamline their workflows, and ensure data governance.

Ontologies give a semantic representation of the data elements within the domain. They can aid the data engineer in understanding how and why data elements are associated and improve processing pipelines. Ontologies also give data scientists context for model development and updating.

The technical and functional attributes of AI systems have been discussed. The next section discusses the different ways to implement systems in a modern cloud context. The use of cloud technology ensures that one can readily scale an AI system based on actual demand and provides for flexibility in resource allocations.

Modern AI deployment paradigms

As AI systems continue to evolve, new deployment paradigms have emerged to address specific requirements and use cases. This section explores two significant approaches: cloud-native AI architectures and edge AI deployments.

Cloud-native AI architectures

The increasing complexity and scale of AI applications have led to the adoption of cloud-native architectures. These architectures leverage the scalability, flexibility, and cost-efficiency of cloud computing platforms to enable efficient development, deployment, and management of AI systems. In a cloud-native architecture, AI components are designed to run seamlessly in cloud environments, taking advantage of specialized services for storage, compute, and networking.

Key characteristics of cloud-native AI architectures include the following:

- **Containerization**: AI applications are packaged into lightweight, portable containers using technologies such as Docker, ensuring consistency across development, testing, and production environments.
- **Orchestration**: Container orchestration platforms such as Kubernetes manage the deployment, scaling, and operation of application containers across clusters of hosts.
- **Microservices**: As discussed earlier, breaking down AI systems into smaller, independent services enables more efficient resource utilization and easier scaling.

- **Serverless computing**: Platforms such as AWS Lambda, Azure Functions, and Google Cloud Functions allow developers to focus on writing code without worrying about the underlying infrastructure, particularly useful for event-driven AI workloads.

- **Managed services**: Cloud providers offer specialized AI services such as fully managed machine learning platforms (e.g., Amazon SageMaker, Microsoft Azure ML, Google Vertex AI) that streamline the development and deployment process.

- **Cloud-native versus lift-and-shift**: Cloud-native AI components are specifically designed to leverage the benefits of cloud environments, such as auto-scaling, serverless computing, and managed services. This approach offers greater flexibility, scalability, and cost-efficiency compared to simply "lifting and shifting" existing on-premises AI systems to the cloud without architectural modifications.

Data lakes and data warehouses in AI architectures: foundations for data-driven intelligence

In the realm of AI, data is the cornerstone of innovation and progress. AI models thrive on massive volumes of data, leveraging it to learn patterns, make predictions, and generate valuable insights. However, effectively managing and harnessing the vast amounts of data involved in AI projects necessitates specialized storage and management solutions. Two prominent concepts that have emerged in this context are **data lakes** and **data warehouses**.

Data lakes: a vast reservoir of raw data

Data lakes serve as expansive repositories where raw data is stored in its native format. They are designed to accommodate structured, semi-structured, and unstructured data from diverse sources. The flexibility of data lakes makes them ideal for storing large volumes of data that may not have a predefined purpose or structure.

- **Key characteristics:**

    - **Schema-on-read:** Data lakes do not enforce a strict schema during ingestion, allowing for flexibility in data types and structures. The schema is defined during analysis or processing, empowering users to adapt to evolving data requirements.

    - **Cost-effective scalability:** Data lakes can easily scale to accommodate growing data volumes, making them a cost-effective solution for storing massive datasets.

- **Support for diverse data:** Data lakes can handle a wide range of data, including sensor readings, social media feeds, log files, and more.
- **Ideal for exploratory analysis:** Data lakes provide a fertile ground for data scientists and analysts to explore data, identify patterns, and generate hypotheses.
- Example use cases:
  - An e-commerce company might store clickstream data, customer reviews, and social media interactions in a data lake for subsequent analysis and personalization efforts.
  - A healthcare organization could use a data lake to store medical images, electronic health records, and genomic data for research and development of AI-driven diagnostic tools.

Data warehouses: structured repositories for analytics

Data warehouses are structured repositories that house processed and curated data, transformed into a consistent format for analysis and reporting purposes. One can build and develop ontologies to organize and provide semantic structure to the data that comes into the system. Ontologies also provide a mechanism to better manage and control model performance by making relationships between data elements explicit.

They excel at facilitating efficient querying and analysis, making them indispensable for business intelligence and decision support applications.

- **Key characteristics:**
  - **Schema-on-write:** Data warehouses enforce a predefined schema during data ingestion, ensuring data consistency and integrity.
  - **Optimized for querying:** Data warehouses employ optimized data structures and indexing techniques to accelerate data retrieval and analysis, enabling faster insights.
  - **Support for structured data:** Data warehouses are primarily designed for structured data, such as transactional data, customer information, and financial records.
  - **Ideal for business intelligence:** Data warehouses empower organizations to generate reports, dashboards, and visualizations for informed decision-making.

- **Example use cases:**

  - A financial institution might use a data warehouse to store transaction data, customer information, and market trends for risk analysis and fraud detection.

  - A manufacturing company could leverage a data warehouse to analyze production data, supply chain metrics, and customer feedback to optimize operations and improve product quality.

The synergy of data lakes and data warehouses

In many AI architectures, data lakes and data warehouses complement each other. Raw data is first ingested into a data lake, where it undergoes cleansing, transformation, and enrichment. The refined data is then transferred to a data warehouse for further analysis and reporting. This synergistic approach enables organizations to leverage the flexibility of data lakes for data exploration and the structure of data warehouses for decision support, creating a robust foundation for data-driven AI applications.

AI on cloud computing: a game-changer for AI

The convergence of AI and cloud computing has opened up a new frontier of possibilities for organizations seeking to leverage the power of AI. Cloud computing provides a scalable, flexible, and cost-effective infrastructure for developing, deploying, and scaling AI applications. By harnessing the capabilities of the cloud, businesses can overcome the limitations of traditional on-premises AI solutions and accelerate innovation.

Benefits of cloud-based AI

Cloud-based AI offers several key advantages that make it an attractive option for organizations of all sizes:

- **Scalability**: Cloud resources can be easily scaled up or down to meet the fluctuating demands of AI workloads. This elasticity allows organizations to handle large datasets, train complex models, and process vast amounts of data without having to invest in and maintain expensive hardware infrastructure.

- **Flexibility**: Cloud platforms provide a wide range of AI services and tools, giving organizations the flexibility to choose the best options for their specific needs. This allows businesses to experiment with different AI approaches, quickly iterate on models, and adapt to changing requirements.

- **Cost-efficiency**: Cloud-based AI can be more cost-effective than on-premises solutions. Organizations only pay for the resources they consume, eliminating the need for upfront capital investments in hardware and software. Additionally, cloud providers often offer pay-as-you-go pricing models, which can further reduce costs.

By leveraging the power of cloud-based AI, organizations can unlock new levels of innovation, efficiency, and competitiveness.

Major cloud AI platforms: accelerating innovation with comprehensive toolsets

Major cloud providers have emerged as key players in the AI landscape, offering comprehensive suites of AI services and tools that cater to a wide range of needs. These platforms provide a one-stop shop for businesses and developers looking to leverage the power of AI in their applications and workflows.

Key cloud AI platforms

- **Google Cloud AI platform (Vertex AI)**: This unified platform streamlines the entire **Machine Learning** (ML) lifecycle, from building and training models to deploying and managing them in production. Vertex AI's AutoML feature simplifies model development for users with limited ML expertise, while the model garden offers a collection of pre-trained models ready for deployment. Vertex AI Pipelines orchestrates complex ML workflows, enabling efficient experimentation and automation.

- **Amazon SageMaker**: A fully managed service, SageMaker empowers users to build, train, and deploy ML models at scale. It boasts a wide array of built-in algorithms and frameworks, making it accessible to both beginners and experienced practitioners. SageMaker's scalability and integration with other AWS services make it a popular choice for enterprise-grade AI solutions.

- **Amazon Bedrock**: This cutting-edge service democratizes access to **Foundation Models** (FMs) from leading AI start-ups and Amazon itself through a simple API. Bedrock enables developers to harness the power of state-of-the-art generative AI capabilities without having to build and train complex models from scratch.

- **Microsoft Azure AI**: This platform offers a diverse range of AI services, including pre-built AI models for computer vision, speech recognition, natural language processing, and decision-making. Azure Machine Learning allows users to create and deploy custom AI models, while the platform's extensive integration with other Azure services makes it a versatile choice for a variety of AI applications.

These cloud AI platforms provide a powerful and accessible way for organizations to incorporate AI into their operations, accelerating innovation and driving business value.

Summary

In this chapter, we have explored the fundamental principles of AI system architecture, establishing a comprehensive framework for understanding the building blocks that power intelligent systems. We examined the core components – data as the lifeblood, algorithmic frameworks that enable learning, model architectures that encapsulate intelligence, and infrastructure that provides computational resources – along with architectural patterns such as microservices that offer modularity and flexibility. Critical design considerations of scalability, performance, reliability, and security were discussed as essential elements for robust AI systems that can grow with increasing demands while remaining resilient and protected.

The landscape of AI deployment continues to evolve rapidly, with cloud-native architectures leveraging containerization, orchestration, and serverless computing to achieve unprecedented efficiency. The synergy between data lakes, data warehouses, and data catalogs creates a solid foundation for data-driven intelligence, while major cloud platforms democratize access to sophisticated AI capabilities. As we move forward, these foundational principles will guide the development of AI systems that are not only powerful but also scalable, reliable, and secure – enabling the next generation of innovations across industries.

Relevant reading

- Bass, Len, Paul Clements, and Rick Kazman. Software Architecture in Practice: Software Architect Practice. Addison-Wesley, 2012.

- Weyns, Danny. Software Architecture: Principles and Practices. MIT Press, 2021.

- Hazelwood, Kim, et al. "Applied Machine Learning at Facebook: A Datacenter Infrastructure Perspective." IEEE International Symposium on **High Performance Computer Architecture (HPCA)**, 2018.

- Sculley, D., et al. "Hidden Technical Debt in Machine Learning Systems." Advances in Neural Information Processing Systems, 2015.

- National Institute of Standards and Technology. "AI Risk Management Framework (AI RMF)." NIST, 2023.

- Baheti, Priya R., and Helen Gill. "Cyber-physical Systems." The Impact of Control Technology, 2011.

- Patterson, David, et al. "Carbon Emissions and Large Neural Network Training." arXiv preprint arXiv:2104.10350, 2021.

- LeCun, Yann, Yoshua Bengio, and Geoffrey Hinton. "Deep Learning." Nature, 2015.

- Mao, Hongzi, et al. "Resource Management with Deep Reinforcement Learning." Proceedings of the 15th ACM Workshop on Hot Topics in Networks, 2016.

2

The Case for Architecture

What would the world look like without civic architecture? Buildings would be built at random, health and safety regulations may not be implemented, there would be no coordination with municipal entities, and the actual time to build would be longer since coordination among the builders would lack an underlying cohesion. The architect, equipped with vision, purpose, processes, tools, and direction, ensures that the right system is built. Rigorously architected systems also allow for a unity of effort and ensure that the whole project team understands what is to be built.

Architecture is also needed for complex systems development. A complex system has many different engineering domains that must come together to build a system that each domain could not do by itself. There are competing demands and incomplete knowledge among all the teams. Many times, there are basic challenges of even knowing how to communicate with each other. In a complex system, there are usually different stakeholders who have demands of the final system that are at odds with each other – an architect must broker these demands.

An architect's role is to develop a unified vision, guide design that is technically achievable, and achieve system creation that meets budget goals and the development schedule.

The role of the architect has roots in antiquity and is pivotal to modern systems. The role of the architect in software systems is just as key as a civil architect. The software architect performs a critical function to ensure the correct system is built and acts as the principal advocate for the end user of the system. The architect is also responsible for ensuring that the system maintains cohesion. This is a tall order. Embracing the role and processes of architecture improves the quality and success of the end system.

Consequences of architectural failures

To start the discussion on architecture for complex software, let's do a quick thought experiment.

Imagine your team is tasked to build an application to conduct queries on a networked data store and return the results to a remote user. Now, you have four software engineers on your team: one who works on the data store, one who works on the service layer, one who integrates the user interface with the data store application, and an engineer who works on the user interface.

Here are seven practices that compromise project success:

1. Undirected communication and coordination among team members, since often there is not a common understanding or reference point to unify action
2. Treating all engineering assumptions as equally valid without requirement validation
3. Making design decisions through majority voting rather than technical expertise
4. Limiting customer communication to user interface engineers only
5. Treating integration and testing as optional activities
6. Eliminating intermediate milestones and review checkpoints
7. Recognizing only the final delivery date as a meaningful project milestone

In this scenario, usable software would not be delivered. Each list item not done would be considered a failure in architecture. This is a simple system – as the demands on the system grow or the domain becomes more challenging, the importance of architecture comes to the fore. AI-enabled software is exceptionally complex software.

This chapter will give some background on the concept of architecture, how it can be used to mitigate failures, and, more importantly, lay out the justification that architecture done right can allow one to deliver robust AI-enabled software.

We will cover the following main topics in this chapter:

- The origins of architecting
- The role of the architect
- The holder of the vision
- Architecting processes
- The language of architecture

The origins of architecting

The profession of architecture has roots in deep antiquity. The word architect comes from the Greek "arche," which means first, and "techion," which means builder. Thus, an architect is the person who brings forth a concept to a system that will serve a purpose. For the modern AI software architect, that means that they must grapple with making a system that can correctly make decisions or inferences in an algorithmic manner.

Ancient architects provided humanity with the pyramids of ancient Egypt, the beautiful structures to honor the Hellenistic gods, and the aqueducts of Rome, to name a few. Egyptian architects conceived and led the development of massive structures that have lasted thousands of years. They were key to the coordination of thousands of workers and the use of mathematics to guide workmanship and the dimensions of rocks, which needed to be cut and placed correctly, with amazing precision and symmetry, thus demonstrating mastery of mathematics and engineering coordination. The architects of the Hellenistic period developed techniques to build temples and structures with beautiful symmetry, utilizing design patterns and making decisions that, though usually not optimal, resulted in a beautiful yet still practical system.

They also coordinated and guided the workmanship and planning to assemble their vision. These structures were massive, and their soundness of structure and load balance have enabled them to last for thousands of years. The Roman architects built amazing coliseums and planned roadways, temples, and aqueducts. This demonstrated the capability to be flexible and have the engineering depth to guide the building of a complex system.

The aqueducts demonstrated a command not only of building structures but also of the use of hydrodynamic principles and advanced engineering to deliver water to many parts of their respective cities. This new type of structure had a transformative effect on cities. Water, as an essential liquid humans need not only for drinking but for cleansing and recreation, could be enjoyed and used by the population.

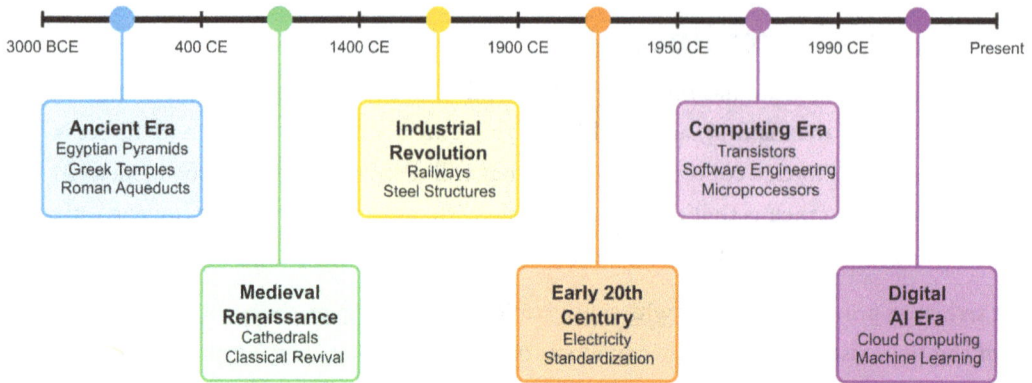

Figure 2.1: Timeline of architectural evolution

🔍 **Quick tip:** Need to see a high-resolution version of this image? Open this book in the next-gen Packt Reader or view it in the PDF/ePub copy.

🔖 **The next-gen Packt Reader** and a **free PDF/ePub copy** of this book are included with your purchase. Scan the QR code OR visit `https://packtpub.com/unlock`, then use the search bar to find this book by name. Double-check the edition shown to make sure you get the right one.

Historically, the architect was usually a single person who drove the vision of the end system to development. The architect is the integrating force that ensures the components that are built come together and realize system-level effects. The insight that architecture is both an ancient and modern art stems from ancient dictums that state that the best systems come from a single vision and that a system should exhibit certain key attributes and the use of design patterns.

With the modern age, specifically the Renaissance period of European history, the continual and accelerating development of technology exploded and has not abated. In the modern world, we have witnessed such breathtaking developments as railways, seafaring vessels, large-scale electricity, automotive vehicles, airplanes, radar, telecommunications, computers, nuclear energy, space flight, medical devices, satellites, the internet, and personal smartphones. A key system that is in its infancy in terms of being an engineering discipline is software. Before going any further, I want to clarify that this is a book on **software architecture** and **AI-enabled systems**. So, going forward, I will use the word *system* in the sense of a *software system*.

Systems architects bridge user needs and technological implementation, orchestrating complex projects through disciplinary coordination, requirement definition, and development oversight.

In AI-enabled systems, architects balance traditional software concerns with specialized challenges:

- Data pipeline management and model development workflows.
- System adaptability while maintaining output stability.
- Integration of algorithmic components with software infrastructure.

Unlike physical structures visualized through drawings, software architecture requires multiple perspectives:

- Logical models and functional specifications.
- Operational scenarios and use cases.
- Interface controls and service agreements.
- Prototypes, simulations, and analyses.

Modern complexity necessitates architectural teams collaborating with domain specialists, while maintaining clear decision authority with a single responsible architect – avoiding the pitfalls of committee-based design decisions.

The role of the architect

What is it that an architect delivers? A derogatory remark is that they are just document creators, since they deliver specifications, concept of operations documents, modeling diagrams, white papers, and technology evaluations. These are artifacts of the architecting process and communication tools that guide follow-on engineering activities. The thinking and collaboration must be done before relevant and impactful documentation is created.

For example, what would happen if a database engineer were only in charge of building an application?

Without a unified vision, specialists naturally optimize according to their expertise – database engineers prioritize data structures while interface designers focus on user experience. This specialization necessitates a central role to provide cohesion. The architect balances customer expectations with technical requirements, guides design decisions, and coordinates project execution.

This section explores the architect's responsibilities, providing insight into the role's breadth and significance. The prestigious title carries substantial responsibility.

From ancient monuments to modern systems, the architect's function remains consistent: satisfying diverse stakeholders while delivering functional solutions. Egyptian pyramid architects balanced ruler glorification with construction feasibility; modern architects similarly reconcile competing priorities while ensuring proper implementation within budget and schedule constraints.

Balancing vision and precision in AI architecture

AI architects must simultaneously function as strategists and technical analysts. Their dual responsibility requires developing value-aligned roadmaps while identifying critical implementation details that could compromise system integrity.

Successful architects employ the 5W+H framework to bridge macro and micro perspectives:

- **Who**: Users, stakeholders, and roles affected by the AI system.
- **What**: Purpose, constraints, technologies, data requirements, and computational complexity.
- **Why**: Justifications for requirements, techniques, and implementation decisions.
- **When**: Delivery timelines, retraining cycles, and integration milestones.
- **Where**: System positioning, data sources, execution environments, and storage solutions.
- **How**: Testing methodologies, integration approaches, error handling, and performance metrics. Also, how to meet non-functional considerations such as security, privacy, historical data stores and overall system observability.

Each inquiry must be evaluated through cost, schedule, and performance lenses while addressing compliance and security constraints. No universal template exists – effective architects apply contextual heuristics, filtering critical details from overwhelming complexity.

AI systems and architecture

AI-enabled systems are implemented in software. Architecture improves the engineering effort by using a host of models, prototyping, reviews, and design guidance. Given the abstract nature of AI-enabled systems, architecting is a risk reduction activity by methodically including many perspectives and engaging stakeholders to ensure first-order mistakes are not made. The architect can define, direct, and evaluate prototyping efforts to ensure that the prototyping is adding value to the project. The use of reviews of documentation and presentations ensures there is cohesive communication across the engineering teams, stakeholders, and end users. This documentation is given to the customer to demonstrate that the engineering efforts are understood and to give the customer the opportunity to impact the direction of the project. The engineering teams use the documentation to aid in executing their respective processes and activities. The documentation aids the project planners with scoping the schedule and budgets for the project. Finally, the documentation is the living document that the architect uses to define and update the final vision of the to-be-built system.

The role of an architect requires them to do the following:

- Understand and define the requirements to the stakeholders.
- Develop models, diagrams, drawings, documents and design artifacts.
- Communicate with builders or engineers such that a builder can actually create the structure or system.
- Oversee and potentially lead the design of a system.
- Coordinate and address issues and problems that occur during development.
- Conduct final acceptance of the built system.

As the progression of technology occurred, the demands on systems have increased exponentially, thus making the architect's role ever more important. For modern systems, there needs to be, as much as is practical, immersion into the domain of stakeholders, such as clients, regulators, partners, and even internal staff. The architect must know how value is going to be created for the customer using the new system. There needs to be an understanding of the various constraints that must be dealt with, such as safety, compliance, and regulatory constraints. A common occurrence is that many software systems fail not so much because any given part of the system was not built or tested correctly, but because the wrong system was built.

The main artifacts of the architect are varied. The architect needs to create and adjudicate system vision documents, guide the full gamut of models, write and communicate specification documents, aid in design reviews, and give guidance for test development programs, verification processes, and ultimately acceptance of the system. The role of the architect is also intertwined with project and program execution.

For AI-enabled systems, architects must do the following:

- Clearly communicate how AI technology delivers value to stakeholders, defining usage and business impact.

- Enable data scientists to build complex models requiring strong mathematical and algorithmic understanding. Standard software diagrams must be augmented with performance simulations, detailed decision mapping, and robust state machine techniques.

- Collaborate closely with AI engineers, ensuring supporting documentation enables unified system operation. The AI engineer looks to integrate machine learning models. They are also tasked with building systems that meet non-functional requirements such that analytic pipelines are scalable, reliable, and controllable. The AI engineer also looks to develop designs that are consistent with the vision of the system. An AI engineer needs to balance their respective detailed designs to conform or not be at odds with the overall vision of the system.

- Identify key non-functional requirements, patterns, and tactics for systems making autonomous decisions without human intervention.

- Guide testing teams through decision correctness verification across varied inputs, including off-nominal scenarios for system robustness.

The architect must lead requirements derivation and use case development to ensure that supporting systems around AI functionality are correctly built.

The holder of the vision

Imagine that you and two friends want to go and eat lunch. For this scenario, you have the final say on where to go, but you must take into full account the desires of your two friends. This simple decision could potentially become involved: What will you eat? Where? What will the cost be? A decision must be made, but how? In this sort of situation, other considerations that impact the decision must be brought forward, such as lifestyle, frugality, allergies, and similar factors. You, as the decider, must craft a decision that synthesizes the desires and limits voiced by your friends. As the one making the decision, you must craft a vision that harmonizes the competing needs of your two friends while ensuring the outcome delivers value. This is what an architect does. They develop a vision for the system and then guide the building of the system in line with the vision. The vision of the system underpins so many aspects of a system that it must be done right, communicated, and ensure it meets the stakeholders' needs.

For AI-enabled systems, architects must articulate how technology delivers stakeholder value, defining clear business impact and usage patterns. Their modeling responsibilities require strong mathematical understanding to create performance simulations, decision mappings, and state machines beyond standard software diagrams.

Architects collaborate with AI engineers, ensuring documentation enables unified system operation. They identify non-functional requirements and architectural patterns for autonomous decision-making without human intervention.

Testing guidance focuses on decision correctness verification across varied inputs and failure scenarios, ensuring system robustness. Throughout development, architects lead requirements derivation and use case development to properly integrate AI functionality with supporting systems.

The architectural cycle

The architectural cycle is an iterative process where analysis, synthesis, and evaluation are done to develop a first-order concept.

Analysis activities include decomposing the major functions and sub-functions that a system needs to provide, the identification of non-functional requirements that are most relevant for the AI-enabled system, and the identification of the driving metrics or measures that can be used to judge the performance of the system or as a measure of other key attributes. Examples of other key attributes can be cost constraints, the time between failures, usability metrics, and so on.

Synthesis activities are a creative process where first-order design is executed to arrive at feasible concepts. This is where the architect can initially use patterns and tactics to describe the logical framework, the identification of processes that must be executed to meet the needs of the customer, and the identification of technologies that can be used.

The evaluation process is executed to sort and prioritize the different synthesized concepts. Modeling and systems analysis can be used to test and understand the bounds of the different concepts. If too much uncertainty or difficulty in evaluation occurs, the use of prototyping may be done to aid this stage. The use of decision matrices can be used. Once a set of concepts is defined, then the final step is to enter into a review process with all the relevant stakeholders, but where the final decision is made by the stakeholder on how to proceed.

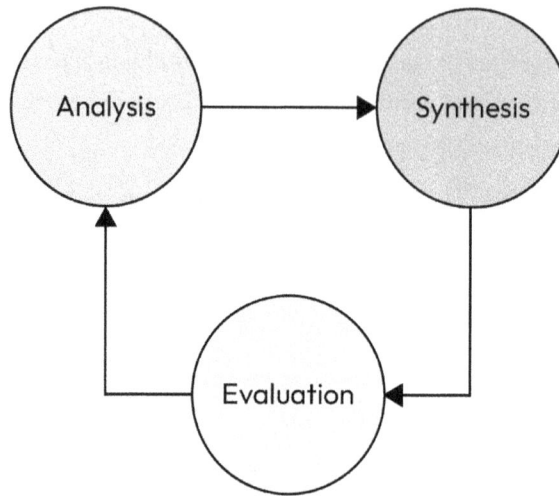

Figure 2.2: Architecture cycle

Thinking like an architect

A common question is how does one think like an architect? This is a skill that can be learned and, with experience, honed. This is especially true if one focuses on a domain or technology approach. A main theme for thinking like an architect is to develop insights into how structures and processes impact the design of the system. For example, the architect should identify or discover the key non-functional requirements of the system. How does the system meet the end goal or main objectives? In software, at a minimum, this requires developing, understanding, and evaluating functions, logical structures, and behavioral processes.

In thinking like an architect, the stakeholders are key, since they are the ones who accept the system and are paying for it to be built. Engagement and validation with stakeholders is gained through interactions, both formal and semi-formal.

Tools to do this include the following:

1. Review of documentation that the customer may already have.
2. Market research on the domain.
3. Inspection or review of competitors of the customer.
4. Interviews, workshops, and focused meetings.
5. Rapid prototyping, constrained demonstrations.
6. The development of key technical documentation with reviews and acceptance by the customer.

Let's use a hypothetical example of thinking like an architect for a financial services domain. Financial institutions must be on constant alert for fraudulent transactions or deception. The use of AI is a great candidate for this type of use case. The challenge for the architect is to decide what type of technology to use from the dozens of approaches that exist. A deep network works very well in identifying off-nominal or odd patterns in transactions, but a deep network cannot give a chain of reasoning for identifying a transaction as required by compliance mandates. A symbolic approach is not as robust as a deep network for identifying off-nominal transactions, but it can provide chain reasoning for classifying a transaction as off-nominal.

What is an architect to do? Consider a logical structure that uses both technologies.

In analyzing the domain, the speed of being able to identify odd situations is a driver. The faster an off-nominal situation is discovered, the faster the downside impacts can be mitigated. The deep net is then used as the first filter, which tags off-nominal conditions to then be fed to a classification engine that would use a symbolic approach.

The following are example questions to be asked to drive architectural considerations:

- What is the inference that drives classification? Lots of activity for an account that was dormant? The size of a transaction?
- What is the data that is going to be coming into the system? Transactions per second? Customer metadata? Outside data sources?
- What is the quality of data that is going to be used? What filtering and transformations need to be done? Does the system need a common time stamp? Do customers need to be anonymized?
- How is the customer's business model impacted by the system? Is this system going to drive revenue increases? Will it lower expenses? Does it meet compliance requirements?
- What is the computing hardware, software, and networking infrastructure needed?
- Is the design intuitive? Who are the staff using it? Junior staff? Accountants? Finance professionals? Operations staff?
- Is the schedule for delivery in line with the customer's funding ability and staff resources to use the technology?
- Can a solution meet cost and schedule constraints?
- What are the new risks that shall be introduced into the customer's organization? Will the system stop transactions? What happens if a transaction is missed?

In thinking like an architect, one gains the big picture and delineates potential key details that could have major architectural consequences.

Maintaining architectural vision

Communicating the system vision to stakeholders is essential, requiring clear articulation of benefits, value, and potential risks. The architect must maintain cohesion throughout development – ensuring consistency while integrating stakeholder feedback and adapting to changing requirements.

Despite inevitable changes, the architect must prevent component and interface divergence to preserve continuity. Stakeholders require a detailed understanding of how the implementation will satisfy functional needs within budget and timeline constraints.

For AI-enabled systems, the vision must address algorithmic decision-making at the system's core. This includes defining appropriate checks and balances, establishing stringent data quality requirements and observability, and designing human-system interactions that build trust in automated operations.

In AI-enabled projects, clearly documenting and communicating the system vision is crucial. It involves collaborative efforts to create key documents and visual aids, which include the following:

- **Concepts of operations documents**: These are especially important in AI projects as they describe how the AI system will operate in various real-world scenarios and how it interacts with users.

- **High-level use case diagrams**: For AI systems, these diagrams are vital as they show the different ways AI will interact with its environment and users, highlighting automated decisions and responses.

- **Logical and functional decompositions**: In the context of AI, these decompositions help stakeholders understand the underlying AI architecture and how different components, such as machine learning models and data processing units, fit together.

- **Support narratives**: These narratives are essential for explaining complex AI functionalities and algorithms in understandable terms, helping non-technical stakeholders grasp how the AI will achieve its intended tasks.

- **Models**: Logical data model artifacts, data flow diagrams, and guidance on data governance approaches.

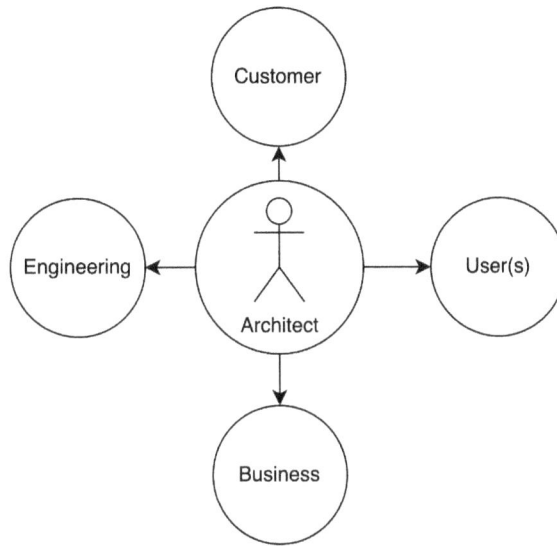

Figure 2.3: Balancing stakeholders

Figure 2.3 gives an overview of how the architect needs to balance the potentially many demands of stakeholders in the development of a vision. To do this effectively, significant communication, diagrams, and engagement must occur. For AI-enabled systems, the architect usually has the most responsibility, being able to communicate and translate how the algorithmic decision-making of the system impacts the stakeholders.

Modern system architecting

What do the systems that delivered humans to the moon and brought them back to earth have in common with advanced medical devices, a modern automobile, and a microprocessor?

They are systems that deliver tremendously specialized capabilities that, before the 20th century, would have been unimaginable. Let's take a short detour to look at how the history of modern system development resulted in the development of architecture.

World War II catalyzed transformative systems – communications, radar, rockets, and nuclear technology – through scientific integration and coordinated engineering. This approach generated hundreds of post-war innovations that revolutionized modern life.

Today's organizations employ systems architects who, like their civil counterparts, create vision, advocate for customers, and drive complex system design. This discipline became essential as performance demands increased across aerospace, electronics, medical, nuclear, and naval domains.

Despite diverse engineering specialties, the need for integrated development remains universal. Complex systems require coordination across numerous teams and stakeholders – unity achieved through architectural models, communications, and artifacts that align diverse disciplines toward cohesive implementation.

For AI-enabled systems, which are the focus of this book, an architect must deal with two significant considerations:

- The use and impact of the AI-enabled components work to meet the customer's needs and performance requirements.
- AI components are usually rooted in complex software systems, so there is non-trivial risk associated with software development.

The fact that a cohesive and consistent architecture for a complex system is needed really is not up for debate. What is up for debate is how one goes about creating an architecture that then drives the system development. A central tenet of the authors is that rigorous architecting is necessary to tame the complexity of modern AI/ML system development and successful deployment.

The execution of software development must involve the availability of source documents from which to scope, trace requirements, guide the design, allow for integration, and ultimately, to conduct testing. The design process requires an overarching set of principles, goals, and constraints so as to build the system, test it, and deploy it. The integration and test teams require insight into what is to be built, so testing resources are allocated and well defined. A whole slew of interrelated documents, governing models, and clear documentation satisfies many of the needs of the key stakeholders of the project. There must also exist a significant verbal and leadership presence to be able to navigate across the different technical teams to ensure design decisions are faithful to the vision, and provide guidance to clarify specifications and validation that a given implementation is the correct one. It is through documentation, presentations, and communications that the architect can ensure a coherent implementation is realized.

There are now standards for software architecture, the most relevant for this audience being IEEE 42010 Systems and software engineering – Architecture description.

Decision-making frameworks for AI architecture

Architecting AI-enabled systems requires a structured decision-making process that balances business objectives, technical feasibility, and ethical considerations. The architect must develop a conceptual foundation for selecting appropriate AI approaches, particularly when working with advanced technologies such as large language models, vector databases, and web search integration.

Selecting the right AI approach

When developing the architectural vision for an AI system, the architect must evaluate which technical path will best serve the business requirements. These generally fall into three categories:

- **Traditional machine learning models**: These are appropriate for systems working with well-structured data and clearly defined problems, such as fraud detection, predictive maintenance, or customer segmentation systems.

- **Deep learning architectures**: These become necessary when dealing with unstructured data requiring complex pattern recognition, including image recognition, natural language processing, or audio processing.

- **Foundation models with retrieval-augmented generation (RAG)**: This modern approach leverages pre-trained foundation models enhanced with domain-specific knowledge retrieval systems. These architectures excel at knowledge-intensive tasks, conversational interfaces, and systems requiring real-time information access.

The selection between these approaches is not merely a technical decision but must be guided by how well each aligns with the overall system vision and stakeholder needs.

Figure 2.4 illustrates the structured decision-making process for AI architecture, showing how business requirements, data characteristics, and quality attributes influence the selection of appropriate AI approaches and infrastructure. The workflow guides architects through defining requirements, analyzing the problem domain, selecting AI technologies, and configuring infrastructure to produce a cohesive architectural blueprint.

Multi-dimensional decision framework

To ensure the architect makes informed decisions that lead to a successful AI implementation, they should evaluate architectural choices across three critical dimensions:

Business alignment

- **Value creation**: How directly will this architecture support revenue generation or cost reduction?

- **Operational efficiency**: What are the ongoing operational costs of maintaining the chosen architecture?

- **Risk profile**: Does this approach introduce compliance, security, or ethical risks that must be mitigated?

Data science considerations

- **Data readiness**: Is sufficient, high-quality data available to support the chosen approach?

- **Performance requirements**: What accuracy, precision, and recall metrics must the system achieve?

- **Model evolution**: How will the architecture support ongoing model updates and fine-tuning?

Technical constraints

- **Computational resources**: What processing power, memory, and storage will the system require?

- **Integration complexity**: How will the AI components interface with existing enterprise systems?

- **Real-time requirements**: What latency constraints must the architecture satisfy?

Structured decision process

To address these multi-dimensional concerns, the architect should implement a structured decision workflow:

1. **Define the vision and requirements**: Establish clear business goals and translate them into functional and non-functional requirements.

2. **Assess the data landscape**: Evaluate available data sources, quality issues, privacy, and potential biases that could impact model performance.

3. **Architecture selection**: Based on requirements and a data assessment, determine which AI approach best balances capabilities with constraints.

4. **Infrastructure planning**: Design the deployment architecture, considering scaling needs, security requirements, and performance constraints.

5. **Prototype and validate**: Develop proof-of-concept implementations to validate key architectural decisions before full implementation.

6. **Implementation strategy**: Create a roadmap for development, testing, and deployment that includes monitoring and feedback mechanisms.

This structured approach ensures that architectural decisions are not made in isolation but are part of a cohesive vision that addresses both technical excellence and business value.

Figure 2.4: Architectural decision flow for AI systems

Balancing innovation and practicality

The architect must strike a balance between leveraging cutting-edge AI capabilities and ensuring system reliability. Novel approaches may offer powerful capabilities but introduce implementation challenges or operational uncertainties. The architect should consider the following:

- **Technological maturity**: Are the chosen technologies production-ready or still experimental?

- **Team capabilities**: Does the organization have the skills to implement and maintain the chosen architecture?

- **Fallback mechanisms**: How will the system handle AI component failures or unexpected behaviors?

By systematically addressing these considerations within a structured decision framework, the architect can develop an AI system architecture that not only meets current needs but can evolve as both business requirements and AI technologies advance.

The language of software architecture

Software architecture communicates the system vision through artifacts, analyses, and synthesis validated by stakeholder engagement. Architects model complex domains using abstractions that organize components, interfaces, and functions for technical planning and execution.

Three essential architectural tools form this language, as described in *Software Architecture in Practice*:

Heuristics reduce complexity through experience-based guidelines:

- Anticipate data corruption and model drift
- Understand mathematical limitations and acceptable errors
- Know computational boundaries and data flow constraints

Tactics solve specific problems:

- Limit data store operations to CRUD functions
- Implement redundant controls for reliability
- Security considerations such as role-based access, encryption, and public key infrastructure

Patterns provide reusable templates:

- Layer functionality to manage complexity
- Structure integrated pipelines for data processing

While newer than traditional engineering disciplines, AI architecture has become critical as intelligent systems form operational foundations, create business value, proliferate in implementation options, establish human trust, and enable human-machine collaboration.

Figure 2.5 shows a mind map of what the authors consider major aspects for the language of architecture.

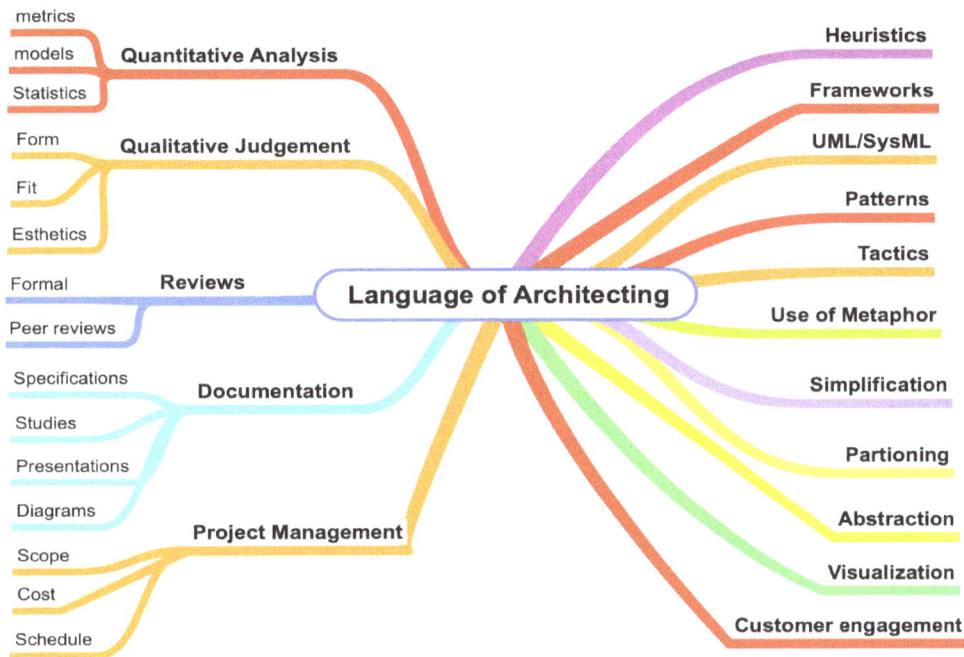

Figure 2.5: Language of architecting

Governance and compliance considerations for AI systems

When developing AI-enabled systems, the architect must address not only functional and performance requirements but also governance, explainability, and compliance dimensions. These aspects represent critical "big picture" concerns that manifest in numerous detailed implementation decisions throughout the system.

Governance framework for AI architectures

AI governance encompasses the policies, procedures, and oversight mechanisms that ensure ethical and responsible AI development. For software architects, this means establishing the following:

- **Bias mitigation strategies:** The architecture must incorporate measurable mechanisms to identify and mitigate bias in both training data and model outputs. This often requires specific model validation components in the pipeline.

- **Accountability structures: Human-in-the-loop** (HITL) mechanisms must be architected into critical decision paths, particularly for high-stakes domains. This means designing explicit points where human review can be done for high-value decision-making under uncertainty.

- **Data provenance tracking**: The system must maintain comprehensive records of data lineage and versioning of data and models, and ensure that all sources used for training and inference comply with data regulations and usage rights.

- **Auditability components**: Logging mechanisms must record model decisions, inference data, and responses in a manner that allows for retrospective review and validation.

Explainability in AI architecture design

Unlike traditional software systems, whose behavior is deterministic, AI systems introduce non-deterministic elements that require special architectural considerations for explainability:

- **Interpretability layers**: For complex models such as deep neural networks, the architect should consider additional components that provide feature attribution, allowing users to understand which inputs most influenced a particular output.

- **Confidence scoring**: AI responses should include confidence metrics to indicate reliability, requiring specific measurement components in the architecture.

- **Decision tracing**: The architecture should enable logging of intermediate steps in AI pipelines, allowing for retrospective analysis and debugging of model behavior.

- **Transparent interfaces**: User interfaces should provide appropriate context for AI-generated content, including citations or explanations of the reasoning process.

Regulatory compliance integration

The architect must ensure that the AI system complies with applicable regulations, which may include the following:

- **Data privacy requirements**: Systems must adhere to regulations such as GDPR (EU) and CCPA (USA), which may necessitate specific components for user consent management, data access controls, and data deletion capabilities.

- **Sector-specific regulations**: In domains such as healthcare (HIPAA) or finance, the architecture must incorporate domain-specific safeguards and documentation.

- **Algorithmic accountability**: Emerging regulations require AI systems to be testable for bias and fairness, requiring the architect to design for comprehensive testing and validation.

Implementation considerations

Consider the following to operationalize governance within AI architectures:

- **Governance dashboards**: Real-time monitoring tools should be integrated to visualize AI decisions, flag anomalies, and track bias metrics.

- **Automated compliance testing**: The architecture should incorporate validation mechanisms that periodically test AI decisions against compliance standards.

- **Federated approaches**: Where privacy concerns are paramount, consider architectural patterns such as federated learning that keep sensitive data decentralized.

- **Explainability-first design**: Rather than treating explainability as an afterthought, it should be integrated at the model development stage.

- **Change control**: Be able to execute rollbacks, failovers, and decision management, such as when to disable non-deterministic decision-making.

By addressing these governance aspects early in the architectural process, the system will be better positioned to meet both technical requirements and ethical standards, ultimately delivering greater value to stakeholders and building user trust.

Modeling and simulation

As with so many other disciplines, software architecture has its own set of tools, concepts, and language. A strong AI architecture effort needs to have a robust and documented set of models.

We will discuss the different types of models that are relevant to this domain and then give some examples of how they would apply to an AI-enabled system.

What is software systems modeling?

Modeling can be thought of as any artifact, analysis, or diagram that can be used to reason about a to-be-built or built system. This impacts the actual design, implementation, integration, testing, and deployment of the software system. Modeling here is taken in a very broad and generic way. For example, it is more than the development of standard modeling from the software engineering community. Examples include the following:

- Unified modeling language models: such as class diagrams, sequence diagrams, and state models.

- Decision trees: a model where the focus is on an algorithmic decision.

- Systems functional chart modeling: processes modeling the business and n-squared diagrams.

- Statistical modeling and data descriptive techniques.

- Analytical-based models: the use of mathematical models that rely on the domain to bound or limit the parameter space of AI technology. For example, if one is developing a technology for vehicle delivery, a kinematic model that limits the speed of a truck on a road is appropriate.

- Data modeling: developing entity-relationship, graph models, and conceptual data models

- User interface mock-ups.

There is specific or more detailed modeling that is applicable to architecting AI/ML systems. These models are more mathematically technical in nature. Examples include the following:

- Descriptive statistical tools to help understand the data inputs, data processing, and results of the AI/ML outputs, such as histograms, box plots, correlation graphs, and correlation matrices.

- The use of hypothesis testing (p-value, statistical significance) is a consideration to benchmark performance or to create bounds on what range and amount of data to be expected. This also aids in developing "circuit breakers" – that is, control logic to ensure that the input data and rates do not adversely impact the performance of AI/ML.

- The use of decision-mapping diagrams or flow charts so as to map out the control paths that can be realized.

The role of modeling and simulation in AI/ML systems

An important aspect of building AI/ML systems is the use of simulations, synthetic data that resembles data being ingested into a production environment, and a simulation is itself a realization of some model. Simulations allow for the testing of the system to see how the actual AI algorithms are performing, but also to get a sense of the performance of the system. The simulation development does not have to be elaborate, but its complexity should mirror to some extent what the target system is looking to do. The simulation requires its own development effort and should be started from the very beginning of the project. In many ways, one grows the simulation as one develops the software of the target system. The simulation acts as both a testing tool and a tool to pose and validate design choices. An application would be to use data with known errors to evaluate the decision logic of the pipeline – for example, collecting temperature data from a low-level, unreliable temperature sensor. One would also use synthetic data to test storage flows and memory management for high-transaction domains, as seen in financial situations. The use of synthetic data can also be used to evaluate model updating upon the detection of model drift, where the domain is dynamic – say, in weather prediction.

The following figure is an overview of the different types of UML diagrams that can be used to model a software system. Not all diagrams need to be created, but a tailoring effort should be done.

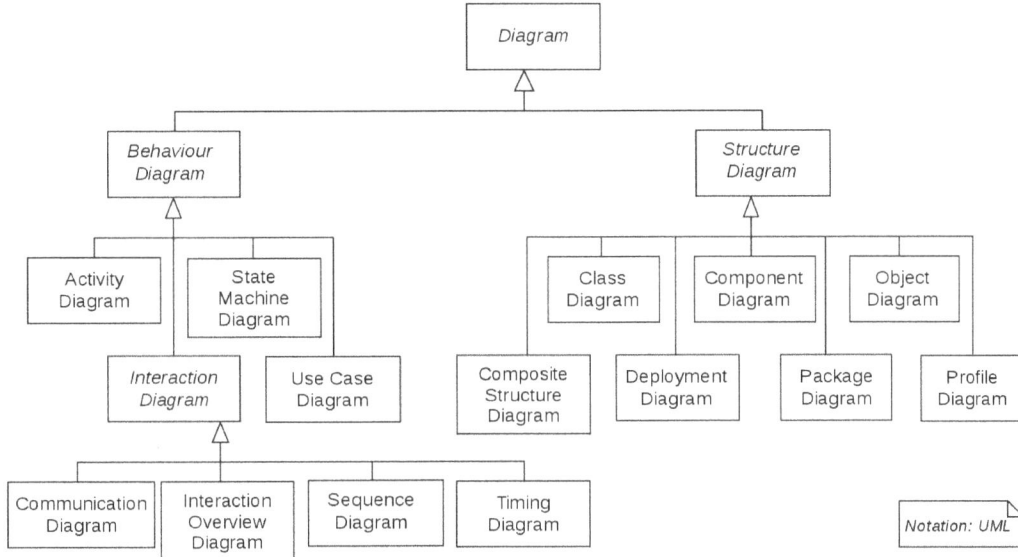

Figure 2.6: Overview of UML diagram types

Architecture and interfaces

An architect works across the technical baseline. They are required to understand how the interacting components integrate through data and control signals. The exchange of data and control signals is realized through interfaces of all sorts, from direct application to application calls, commands from a user interface, and web services. Since the architect has this larger perspective, they are a principal authority on the creation, updating, and retiring of interfaces.

Interfaces

A final note on the nature of interfaces and the role that interfaces have in software engineering. Very rarely in a software system is all the needed data and functionality encased in one area of the code base. Normally, for a subsystem to meet its requirements, it needs data from another part of the system.

In general, when one looks at a logical or functional model of a software system, connecting lines usually indicate either an exchange of data, the flow of a decision, or both. Interface engineering is critical for system cohesion so that a given development team's need to change a key piece of functionality does not inadvertently cause errors in other parts of the architecture. Also, many times, what one system considers "raw data" is processed "metadata" from another system. The mechanism to ensure cohesion in the system is to implement interface engineering. Interface engineering is needed to get data to the right place, at the right time, in the right way, and in the right format. More than any other role, interfaces should be controlled and directed by the architecture team.

Interfaces and AI

Data interfaces primarily impact the processing pipeline and algorithmic decision-making components. This core functionality cannot conduct all possible verification and validation techniques. So, it must trust that the component sending it data conforms to the interface design in terms of format, scale, timing, and correctness. Interfaces are critical to ensure there is "model integration." That is, as the algorithmic decisions are made, the outputs drive follow-on functionality. Interface engineering ensures that the intent of the decision is correctly executed and in a manner consistent with the engineering requirements of the overall system.

Summary

In conclusion, an argument has been made that conducting methodical and rigorous architecting is an enabler for the development and deployment of a successful AI system. Developing an architecture will almost certainly lower overall costs, allowing you to meet the schedule and achieve the desired end performance. One needs to hold back on the temptation that there is too much schedule pressure, so that coding needs to start "right now." In the next chapter, we bring together this more abstract discussion as to how it impacts software engineering specifically.

Relevant reading

- Bass, L., Clements, P., & Kazman, R. (2012). *Software Architecture in Practice*. Addison-Wesley Professional.

- Rechtin, E., & Maier, M. W. (2010). *The Art of Systems Architecting* (3rd ed.). CRC Press.

- Weyns, D. (2021). *Software Architecture: Principles and Practices*. MIT Press.

- International Council on Systems Engineering. (2015). *INCOSE Systems Engineering Handbook: A Guide for System Life Cycle Processes and Activities* (4th ed.). Wiley.

- Kruchten, P. (1995). Architectural Blueprints—The "4+1" View Model of Software Architecture. *IEEE Software, 12*(6), 42-50.

- Baheti, P. R., & Gill, H. (2011). Cyber-physical Systems. *The Impact of Control Technology*, 161-166.

- Sculley, D., Holt, G., Golovin, D., Davydov, E., Phillips, T., Ebner, D., Chaudhary, V., Young, M., Crespo, J. F., & Dennison, D. (2015). Hidden Technical Debt in Machine Learning Systems. *Advances in Neural Information Processing Systems*, 2503-2511.

- Hazelwood, K., Bird, S., Brooks, D., Chintala, S., Diril, U., Dzhulgakov, D., Fawzy, M., Jia, B., Jia, Y., Kalro, A., Law, J., Lee, K., Lu, J., Noordhuis, P., Smelyanskiy, M., Xiong, L., & Wang, X. (2018). Applied Machine Learning at Facebook: A Datacenter Infrastructure Perspective. *IEEE International Symposium on High Performance Computer Architecture (HPCA)*, 620-629.

3

Software Engineering and Architecture

AI-enabled software represents a significant leap in system complexity. Unlike traditional software that follows deterministic rules, AI-enabled software attempts to mimic human decision-making, reasoning, and goal-seeking through heuristic algorithmic means. In doing so, creating multidimensional complexity and, hence, a non-deterministic system. There are different types of challenges to address than traditional software engineering.

This complexity manifests in various ways, from the integration of specialized machine learning components to the need for robust data pipelines, from handling model uncertainty to ensuring appropriate human oversight. Consider the sobering statistic from Gartner that, through 2022, 85% of AI projects delivered erroneous outcomes due to bias in data, algorithms, or the teams responsible for managing them [1]. This highlights the critical importance of robust architecture in AI system development.

To comprehend the scale of complexity we're discussing, consider that the Linux operating system had over 30.34 million lines of source code as of 2021 (www.kernel.org). Linux powers millions of computers, from mission-critical systems to hobby kits, and was built by thousands of engineers working in self-organized groups over several decades. That such a complex system functions reliably is a modern marvel, made possible through a stable and modular architecture that frames system development.

> *"Complexity is the business we are in, and complexity is what limits us."*
>
> *Frederick Brooks, The Mythical Man-Month*

Architecture in software shares common elements with other engineering domains such as civil, aerospace, and medical, though each field implements different models, patterns, and decompositions. The core goal remains consistent: ensuring the correct system is built. For complex software, especially AI-enabled systems, a disciplined architectural approach is essential to simplify the problem space and scope technical solutions through abstraction and modeling.

In this chapter, we'll explore how software becomes complex in AI systems, outline architecting processes and documentation that mitigate these complexities, and examine the role of architects in project management to ensure successful project completion.

Understanding software complexity in AI systems

Several distinct but interdependent types of software complexity exist in AI-enabled systems. Architecture serves as a tool to manage this complexity through modeling, which helps the architecture team reason about the system and provides a foundation for detailed specifications and team communication.

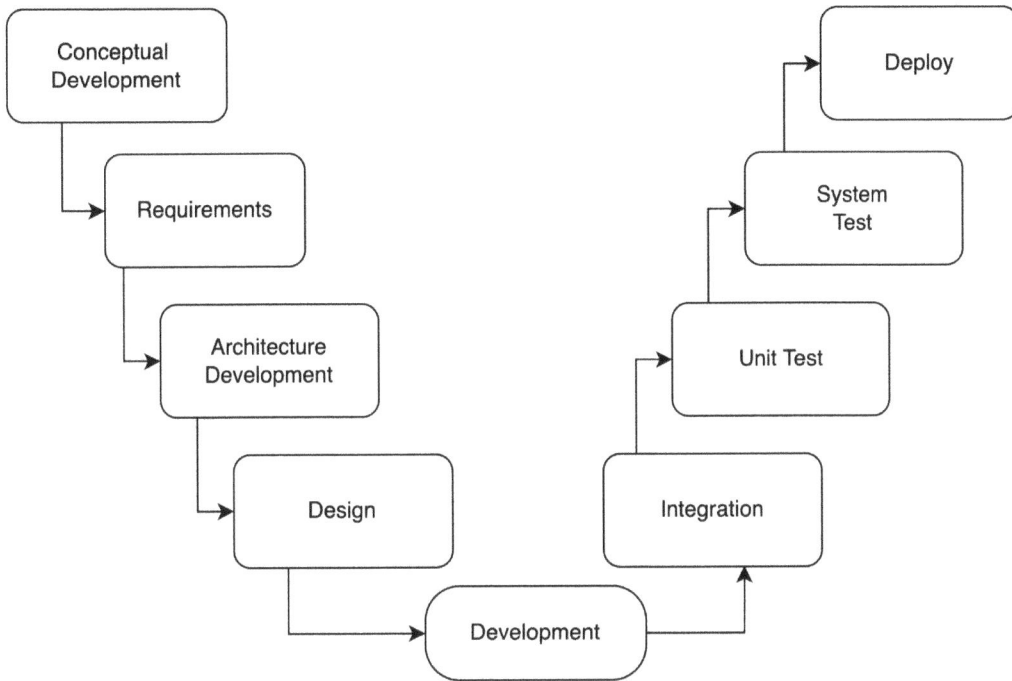

Figure 3.1: Software development lifecycle for AI systems

As shown in *Figure 3.1*, the development process for AI systems follows a structured lifecycle that begins with conceptual development, then moves through requirements gathering and architecture development before proceeding to design and development. After development, the process continues with integration, unit testing, system testing, and finally deployment. This systematic approach helps manage the inherent complexities of AI systems by ensuring that architectural considerations are addressed early in the development process. An excellent resource for learning about systems methodology can be found in the *INCOSE Systems Engineering Handbook* [5]. The authors posit that this sort of cycle can be applied to different development methodologies, be it a waterfall development or Agile methodology.

Integration complexity

Software integration becomes particularly challenging when development teams must incorporate code bases they didn't create or don't control. This spans multiple layers of the software stack, from operating system kernels to application frameworks. These different software packages have varying dependencies on libraries, operating systems, versions, and programming languages.

For AI-enabled systems, it's economically advantageous to leverage open source or commercial packages for core algorithms rather than building functionality from scratch. We see this in the widespread adoption of frameworks such as TensorFlow, PyTorch, and scikit-learn, which provide ready-made implementations of complex machine learning algorithms. Consequently, the rest of the software architecture often needs to adapt to accommodate these components.

Case study: healthcare AI integration

A healthcare provider implementing a diagnostic assistance system faced significant integration challenges when incorporating a pre-trained deep learning model for medical image analysis. The model, built with TensorFlow, required specific versions of supporting libraries that conflicted with the hospital's existing Java-based infrastructure. The architecture team solved this by implementing a microservice architecture with containerized components, allowing the AI system to operate in an isolated environment while communicating with existing systems through well-defined APIs. This said, there also exists the complexity of API management. This includes working with updated or revised APIs. This then forces the version control and compatibility of APIs based on the evolution of models or the application itself.

Functional complexity

The need for autonomous decision-making or inference introduces significant functional complexity. The decision process must be executed correctly for the system to fulfill its objectives. This requires implementing robust checks through monitoring, alerts, and alarms, as human oversight isn't always available to ensure decision correctness.

AI technologies also introduce requirements for model re-training and deployment when models become incorrect or outdated. Alert systems and break points must be implemented to allow human override when the system operates incorrectly. Additionally, extensive logging is necessary to enable checking, alerting, and diagnostic functionality.

Privacy concerns and management of large volumes of log data become particularly important in AI systems that involve sensitive data, such as those in healthcare, finance, or government applications. A well-architected system must include mechanisms for data anonymization, secure storage, and controlled access to logs.

Technical complexity

AI algorithms place tremendous demands on underlying hardware. The computational complexity of algorithms, data preprocessing needs, and performance margins add complexity to hardware deployment decisions. As an example, training a large language model such as GPT-3 required approximately 3.14×10^{23} FLOPS of compute [2], highlighting the extreme computational demands of modern AI systems.

Timeliness requirements for query and data processing introduce additional challenges. In real-time applications such as autonomous vehicles or financial trading systems, AI components must deliver decisions within strict time constraints, requiring careful optimization of the entire processing pipeline.

Processing pipelines require careful consideration of volatile memory and data storage needs. For instance, a computer vision system processing high-resolution images might generate terabytes of intermediate data that must be efficiently managed. Additionally, cybersecurity requirements add another layer of complexity through monitoring, encryption, and logging needs.

Scalability becomes a critical concern as AI systems move from development to production. The architecture must account for increasing data volumes, user loads, and computational demands, often requiring distributed computing approaches and cloud-based infrastructure.

Verification complexity

Ensuring the correct implementation of algorithms and test cases presents unique challenges in AI systems. Unlike traditional software, where outputs are deterministic, AI systems produce probabilistic results that can vary based on training data, initialization parameters, and even random factors introduced during training.

For AI components, understanding and defining nominal or unexpected data inputs is essential to demonstrate system robustness. This involves testing with adversarial examples, edge cases, and out-of-distribution data to ensure the system behaves appropriately even when faced with unfamiliar inputs.

While unit testing is valuable, integration testing often reveals failures that unit tests miss. A subtler verification challenge involves ensuring all logic paths and potential execution paths are adequately tested, which becomes exponentially more difficult in AI systems with complex decision boundaries.

Example: verification in computer vision

Consider a pedestrian detection system for autonomous vehicles. Unit tests might verify that the model correctly identifies pedestrians in a test dataset with high accuracy. However, integration testing might reveal that the system fails when camera inputs are affected by adverse weather conditions or unusual lighting. Even more concerning, adversarial testing might show that specific patterns on clothing could cause the system to miss detecting pedestrians entirely. Robust verification must account for all these scenarios.

Human interface complexity

The roles and interactions between users and AI functionality must be clearly understood. This defines how information, warnings, alerts, and alarms will be activated, presented, and acted upon within the overall system.

The concept of levels of automation, as developed by Parasuraman et al. [3], provides a framework for understanding the division of responsibilities between human users and automated systems. Even highly autonomous AI systems require human configuration, oversight, and intervention capabilities.

If conflicts arise between user commands and AI system recommendations, the system must have clear protocols for adjudication. Similarly, the approach for user involvement in AI learning frameworks for model updates or improvements must be well-defined.

Explainability is a critical aspect of human interface design in AI systems. Users need to understand why an AI system made a particular recommendation or decision, especially in high-stakes domains such as healthcare, finance, and legal applications. This requires thoughtful design of explanation mechanisms that bridge the gap between complex mathematical models and human understanding.

Architecting in practice

Complex software systems are rarely built from scratch, and architects typically don't have complete command of all relevant technologies or domain expertise. This necessitates an architecting function distributed across a small team that typically includes the key roles called out in *Figure 3.2*.

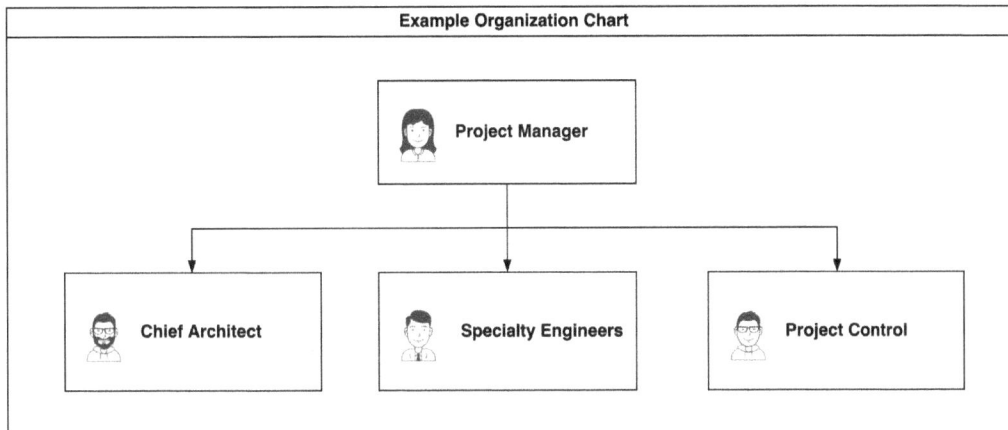

Figure 3.2: Example organization chart for AI project teams

🔍 **Quick tip**: Need to see a high-resolution version of this image? Open this book in the next-gen Packt Reader or view it in the PDF/ePub copy.

📖 **The next-gen Packt Reader** and a **free PDF/ePub copy** of this book are included with your purchase. Scan the QR code OR visit https://packtpub.com/unlock, then use the search bar to find this book by name. Double-check the edition shown to make sure you get the right one.

As illustrated in *Figure 3.2*'s organizational structure, AI project teams typically have the Project Manager at the top, with three key roles reporting directly to them: the Chief Architect, Specialty Engineers such as data engineers, data scientists, user interface developers, full stack developers, DevOps engineers, security engineers, operations analysts, compliance analysts, and project control analysts. This structure ensures that architectural concerns are given proper weight in project decisions, with the Chief Architect playing a crucial role in translating business requirements into technical specifications. Some key roles are outlined here:

- **Vision Holder**: This role focuses on the end customer's needs and communicates the vision through technical documentation, presentations, diagrams, and working-level meetings. For AI systems, this role must understand both business objectives and the capabilities and limitations of AI technologies.

- **Technology Expert**: This role provides a specific understanding of the major components needed in the software system, including database technologies, middleware, user interface design, computational requirements, networking, and storage needs. In AI systems, this expertise extends to machine learning frameworks, model deployment technologies, and data management systems.

- **AI Engineer**: This role understands the data science or analytics process to ensure AI components meet the architectural vision and operate within technology constraints while delivering value to the end customer. This includes knowledge of machine learning algorithms, data preparation techniques, and model evaluation metrics.

The domain knowledge and AI/ML engineering roles should be tightly coupled since the ultimate goal is for AI/ML technology to deliver unique value to end customers. These functions come together to document and communicate the system vision.

A general rule of thumb from the systems engineering community is that architecting types of efforts should consume approximately 12–15% of project resources [5]. While this might seem unproductive initially, this up-front work saves time and prevents major technical errors later in the project, particularly in AI systems where architectural decisions can have far-reaching implications for system performance, maintainability, and scalability.

Approaches for taming software complexity

The most visible artifacts from the architecting process are interrelated documents that guide system development. These include concept of operations documents, use cases, activity diagrams, logical diagrams, non-functional requirements specifications, metrics definitions, and the identification of software development tactics and patterns.

Developing the architecture

Even the smallest projects should develop a **Concept of Operations (CONOPS)** document that justifies the AI-enabled system and explains how users will interact with it. The CONOPS document should describe how users will utilize the AI aspects of the system, how AI will be presented to customers, and how customers can impact AI decisions or outputs.

This document will also identify the major actors involved with the system and how AI/ML components will interact with them, if at all. The CONOPS document should delineate other systems that the AI system will interface with and how it fits into the larger system of systems. A recommended standard is the IEEE standard 1362-1998, "IEEE Guide for Information Technology — System Definition — **Concept of Operations (ConOps)** document."

Another set of key artifacts developed by the architect is the description of the system through diagrams from the **Unified Modeling Language (UML)** or **System Modeling Language (SysML)**. Not all UML or SML diagrams need to be developed.

The most common diagrams include the following:

1. **UML use case diagrams**: Identify actors, roles, and actions that create value
2. **SysML block definition diagrams**: Capture the major logical components of the system
3. **SysML activity diagrams**: Show general flow of control
4. **UML state transition diagrams**: Capture system states and transitions
5. **SysML interface control documents**: Define data exchanges between components
6. **IDEF0 diagrams**: Show inputs, objectives, constraints, and outputs of AI/ML decisions

These diagrams must capture the full cycle of AI/ML functionality, capturing decision-making processes. These diagrams should capture major logic decisions, error-handling approaches, model maintenance, validation, and re-training processes. Additionally, diagrams should show human interactions and control of the overall system. They should highlight key data engineering aspects, including data cleansing, transformation, and quality checks.

The data exchange interface is particularly critical for AI systems, defining how data exchange will be executed, including quality checks, volume, rates, and formats. This interface management and service-level agreements for data exchanges are part of data engineering, ensuring the system can be scalable, resilient, and perform within computational constraints. In the following chapters, more details and examples of these diagrams are presented.

As described by Bass et al. [4], software architecture is driven by non-functional requirements levied on the system. Examples include reliability, scalability, and usability. For AI/ML systems, common non-functional requirements include the following:

1. **Reliability**: How the system handles failures and maintains operation
2. **Explainability**: How the system explains its decisions and recommendations
3. **Fairness**: How the system ensures equitable treatment across user groups
4. **Privacy**: How the system protects sensitive data
5. **Adaptability**: How the system evolves as data patterns change

Understanding and defining these requirements for AI/ML components is essential for successful system development.

Integration and cohesion

Complex AI/ML software systems require team development, demanding robust integration approaches established before integration activities begin. The architecture team doesn't need complete implementation details, but must guide the process effectively.

Four main integration activities are as follows:

1. **Design adequacy assessment**: Determining whether the design meets functional and non-functional requirements
2. **Non-functional requirements evaluation**: Assessing how well the system satisfies quality attributes
3. **Metrics measurement**: Initial determination of key system performance indicators
4. **Interface verification**: Ensuring interfaces are correctly implemented and used

The architect must understand how different system components and data engineering impact the overall system. Integration issues inevitably arise, and the architect must carefully evaluate the impact of requirement changes across the system.

For example, a seemingly simple change in a database query response time could cause an AI component to receive out-of-sync data, leading to incorrect decisions. The architect must identify and address such dependencies early in the development process.

Integration typically is the first time non-functional requirements are tested. Addressing architectural-level issues early in the development lifecycle is critical. Late-stage architectural changes can have significant cascading effects on the system. Integration also provides the first opportunity to measure key system metrics and test interfaces between components. There exist several mechanisms and processes that help address integration challenges. The use of DevOps **continuous integration/continuous deployment (CI/CD)** techniques allows for the testing of new code in an automated way. This automation has steps set up where pre-defined integration testing happens as new code is developed and merged into the configured pre-production system baseline. The use of DevOps also allows for change management to identify areas of the baseline that were changed and are causing integration errors. Another advantage of a DevOps process is the rollback of a baseline in the event of an issue or undesired behavior from a production release.

Project management

The architect plays a crucial role in project management, though they shouldn't be the project manager due to other responsibilities. The architect contributes to the five major project management activities defined by the Program Management Institute in the Program Management Book of Knowledge:

Project initiation

The architect helps develop key documents, including objectives, statement of work, work breakdown structure, schedule, and other project management documents. They clarify work scope, define milestones, and identify necessary resources, including staff type, level of effort, and supporting materials. Depending on the size of the project or the engineering culture of the organization, a system engineering team may exist. If this team is present, they work closely with the architect, identifying key features and work planning—for example, in an Agile development methodology, they aid in the creation of epics and user stories.

The architect also provides input on project execution methodology, such as Agile or spiral approaches.

TO DO	DOING	DONE
Task 1 *New*	**Task 4** *In progress*	**Task 6** *Completed*
Task 2 *New*	**Task 5** *In progress*	**Task 7** *Completed*
Task 3 *New*		**Task 8** *Completed*

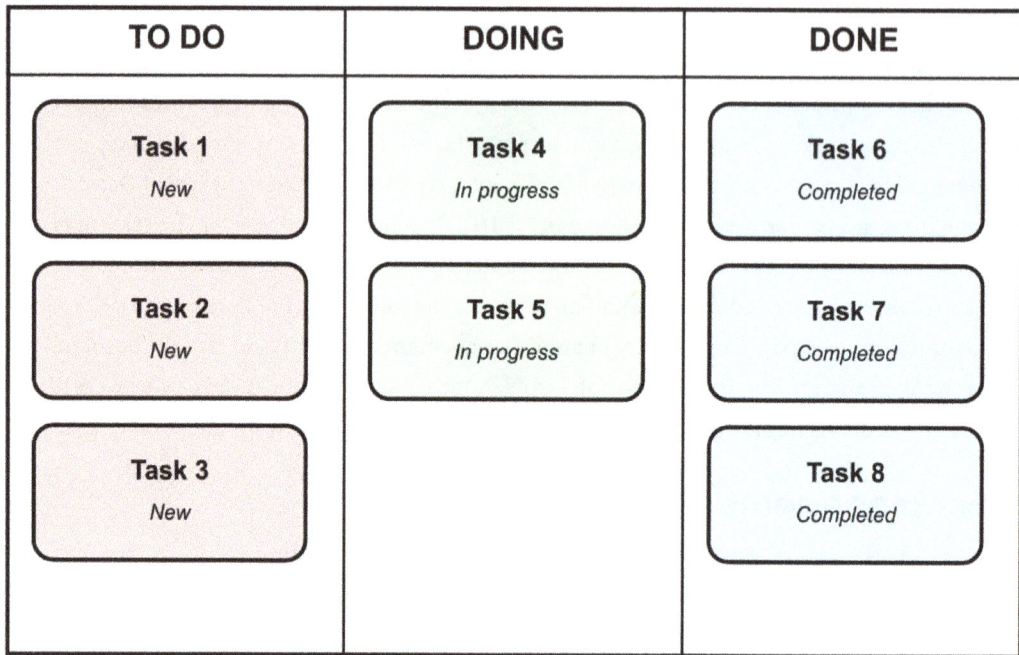

Figure 3.3: Kanban board for Agile AI development

For AI projects, an Agile methodology such as Kanban (shown in *Figure 3.3*) often works well, allowing for a continuous flow of tasks and software development as models are refined and improved through iteration. The Kanban board visualizes work in three columns: *TO DO* for tasks that haven't been started, *DOING* for tasks currently in progress, and *DONE* for completed tasks. There are other methods of organizing a Kanban board, with more stages. The authors chose to highlight the most basic type of board. Tasks can occur over a single or several execution cycles. In Agile, this is called a "sprint."

Example activities to meet the criteria of "Done" in a sprint are as follows:

1. There has been a code review
2. Unit testing has been conducted
3. The new code has been run through the CI/CD pipelines
4. Human acceptance testing

An important note is that a feature may require several tasks over a longer period to be considered "Done." The use of documentation and guidance from the architect aids in tracking and validation that a multi-sprint task is considered "Done."

This visual management tool helps teams track progress and identify bottlenecks in the development process, which is particularly valuable for AI projects where tasks may have varying levels of complexity and uncertainty.

Project planning

During planning, the architect identifies major milestones and technical evidence requirements for milestone completion. They help determine team composition, effort allocation, and financial planning. The architect establishes reporting requirements and configuration control strategies for the architecture team.

For AI systems, planning must account for the iterative nature of model development, the uncertainty in algorithmic performance, and the need for continuous data collection and quality assurance.

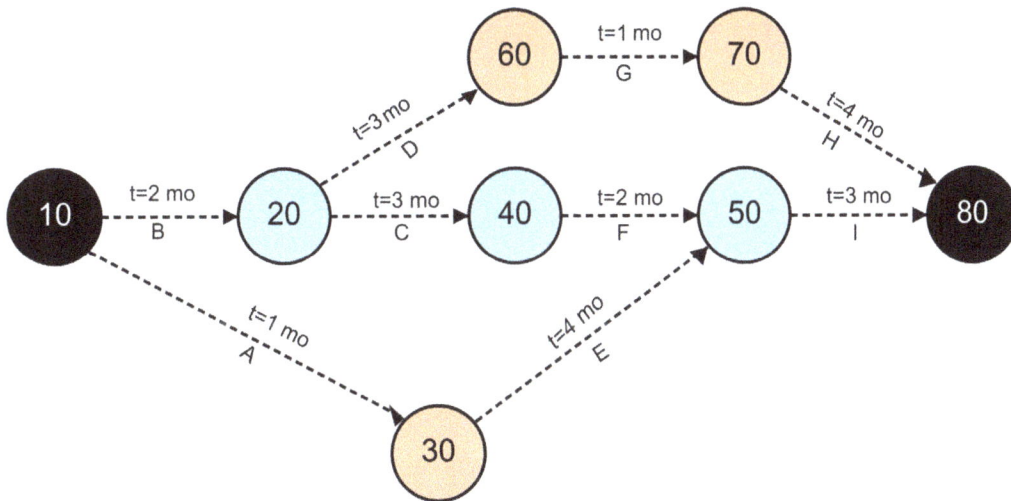

Figure 3.4: Critical path analysis for AI system development

This planning process often involves critical path analysis, as depicted in *Figure 3.4*, which shows how different activities and dependencies affect the overall project timeline. In this network diagram, nodes represent project milestones (numbered 10 through 80), while edges represent activities (labeled A through I) with their associated durations (t=1 mo to t=4 mo). The critical path analysis helps project managers and architects identify which activities must be completed on time to prevent project delays, as well as which activities have slack time that can be utilized if resources need to be reallocated.

Project execution

In execution, the architect oversees work items allocated to their team and supports other engineering teams by providing insights and clarifications. They help the project manager track overall project execution and ensure integration activities will produce a coherent system.

The architect serves as a key resource for resolving technical conflicts, clarifying requirements, and ensuring design decisions align with the overall vision. This role becomes particularly important in AI systems where trade-offs between model accuracy, computational efficiency, and explainability must be carefully balanced.

Monitoring and control

For monitoring and control, the architect provides quality checks and reviews of engineering efforts, giving the project manager updates on schedule and resource utilization. The architect helps interpret technical progress and identify potential risks before they impact project outcomes.

In AI projects, monitoring extends to tracking model performance metrics, data quality, and drift detection to ensure the system continues to meet requirements as it operates in the real world.

Project closing

In the closing phase, the architect ensures testing and certification are complete, advocating for the customer during final system validation. They work with the project manager on system deployment and delivery, providing the key artifacts required by the contract and statement of work.

For AI systems, closing activities might include knowledge transfer of model maintenance procedures, handover of monitoring tools, and documentation of future improvement opportunities.

Case study: AI project management in action

A financial services company implementing a fraud detection system using machine learning faced significant project management challenges. The initial project plan, based on traditional waterfall software development approaches, failed to account for the iterative nature of model development and the complexity of integrating with existing transaction processing systems.

The architecture team restructured the project using an Agile methodology around three-week sprints, with each sprint focusing on improving specific aspects of model performance while gradually expanding integration points. A key point of Agile methodology advocates the development of features in an iterative manner to get quick and impactful feedback from stakeholders. Also, by getting working code delivered sooner, the system could be tested and validated in a quicker manner, reducing total development time. They implemented early integration testing using synthetic data, allowing parallel development of both model components and system interfaces. This approach enabled them to identify and address integration issues early, ultimately delivering a system that reduced fraud losses by 37% while meeting all compliance requirements.

The authors do not intend to advocate for just an Agile methodology. Advantages of waterfall mechanisms are: robust requirements elicitation is done, and project control is more closely tracked through schedule definition and oversight of resources. Also, usually, time is allocated for robust documentation. Disadvantages of Agile methods are: a major function or interface is not accounted for, and Agile methods can lose architectural coherence. This happens when too much parallel development enables the execution of conflicting major design decisions. That said, we think that Agile methods with architecting aspects as described in this text are more effective in developing complex AI systems.

Summary

In this chapter, we discussed how algorithmic decision-making in AI systems introduces unique forms of software complexity. We identified several dimensions of this complexity—integration, functional, technical, verification, and human interfaces—and explained how architecting processes and documentation applied early in the development project can help manage these challenges.

AI-enabled systems are not merely traditional software with an AI component bolted on; they represent a fundamentally different class of system that requires thoughtful architecture to achieve their potential. The role of the architect in these systems extends beyond technical design to include project management, stakeholder communication, and ensuring that the final system delivers the intended value.

As we progress through this book, we'll build on these foundational concepts to explore specific AI techniques, implementation examples, and detailed architecting processes and development artifacts. These tools will equip you to successfully navigate the complexities of AI system development and create robust, valuable solutions that effectively leverage AI capabilities.

It is the position of the authors that architecting is best learned by doing. As one conducts more architecting tasks and projects, one can hone their skills. The following are some exercises that are done on different types of systems and will aid in the development of architecting skills.

Exercises

1. Identify several component and process architecture products for an AI/ML system.

2. Research and identify how CONOPS and requirements documents are used and integrated.

3. Identify the major components of a complex website—such as Amazon, Google Maps, Zillow, or other systems where many components need to be integrated.

References

1. Gartner, "Gartner Says Nearly Half of CIOs Are Planning to Deploy Artificial Intelligence," February 2018.

2. Brown, T., et al., "Language Models are Few-Shot Learners," Advances in Neural Information Processing Systems, 2020.

3. Parasuraman, R., Sheridan, T.B., and Wickens, C.D., "A model for types and levels of human interaction with automation," IEEE Transactions on Systems, Man, and Cybernetics-Part A: Systems and Humans, vol. 30, no. 3, pp. 286-297, 2000.

4. Bass, L., Clements, P., and Kazman, R., "Software Architecture in Practice," Addison-Wesley, 2012.

5. International Council on Systems Engineering, "INCOSE Systems Engineering Handbook: A Guide for System Life Cycle Processes and Activities," 4th Edition, 2015.

Part 2

Architecting AI Systems

The second part of the book walks you through more detailed explanations, guides, and lessons learned to build AI-enabled systems. This part of the book starts with conceptual design, one of the most critical phases led by an architect. The final chapters of this section go into more detail on the architect's role in going from conceptual design to system testing. Finally, a case study is highlighted as a real and common challenge where an AI-enabled system can readily transform a business problem.

The following chapters are included in this section:

- *Chapter 4, Conceptual Design for AI Systems*
- *Chapter 5, Requirements and Architecture for AI Pipelines*
- *Chapter 6, Design, Integration, and Testing*
- *Chapter 7, Architecting a Generative AI System – A Case Study*

4

Conceptual Design for AI Systems

Imagine walking into a restaurant where the waiter immediately tells you what you'll eat without offering a menu, asking about your preferences, or discussing your budge – yet you're still expected to pay. Such a restaurant would quickly fail. What's missing? Customer engagement to understand actual needs and a mechanism for feedback. This scenario parallels what happens too often in complex software development, particularly with AI-driven systems [1].

By conducting thorough conceptual design activities, we mitigate the risks of misunderstanding user and stakeholder needs. The artifacts developed during this phase provide architects with a perspective on the system's end goals and constraints and how customers perceive value. Conversely, these artifacts allow customers to concretize their objectives, surface major implicit assumptions, communicate with other stakeholders, and gain confidence that system builders understand their desires.

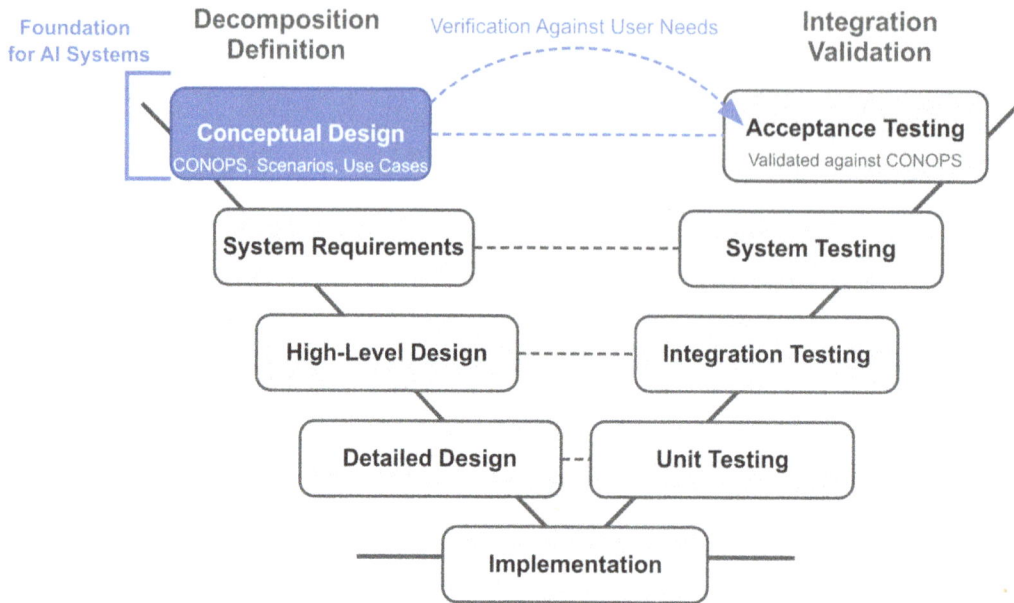

Figure 4.1: Conceptual design in the system engineering "V" model

🔍**Quick tip**: Need to see a high-resolution version of this image? Open this book in the next-gen Packt Reader or view it in the PDF/ePub copy.

🔖**The next-gen Packt Reader** and a **free PDF/ePub copy** of this book are included with your purchase. Scan the QR code OR visit https://packtpub.com/unlock, then use the search bar to find this book by name. Double-check the edition shown to make sure you get the right one.

As illustrated in *Figure 4.1*, conceptual design forms the foundation of the systems engineering "V" model. This model shows how conceptual design serves as the starting point that influences all subsequent stages of development and how the system is ultimately validated against these initial concepts. For AI systems in particular, proper conceptual design is critical to mitigate the exponentially increasing costs of misalignment, especially considering the complex data dependencies these systems entail.

The key learning outcome for this chapter is understanding that conceptual design provides the first pillar in formulating the system vision. Proper conceptual design mitigates the risk of building the wrong system – a risk that becomes exponentially more costly with AI-driven systems due to their data dependencies and complex interactions.

The conceptual design artifact comprises the concepts of the operations document, scenarios, and use cases. This artifact serves multiple purposes: it gives end users and funding customers a mechanism to discuss key activities, objectives, constraints, and performance expectations. It also becomes the starting point for more detailed technical activities that guide system development throughout the engineering "V."

In this chapter, we are going to discuss the following:

- Concept of operations
- The business case for AI systems
- Roles, scenarios, and use cases in AI-enabled systems

Concept of Operations (CONOPS)

What would happen if, when building a house, no plans existed to guide the carpenters in framing the structure? The result would be mass confusion and an almost guaranteed project failure. Building complex software systems, especially those incorporating AI and ML components, is no different. The architect must not only develop a vision for the system but also document it thoroughly so that subsequent efforts can be executed, coordinated, and planned effectively.

The **Concept of Operations (CONOPS)** is precisely such a document. Within conceptual design, the CONOPS acts as the initial definition of the system-to-be. It provides key stakeholders with insights into what the final system will do, how well it should perform, key constraints, and what it should not do.

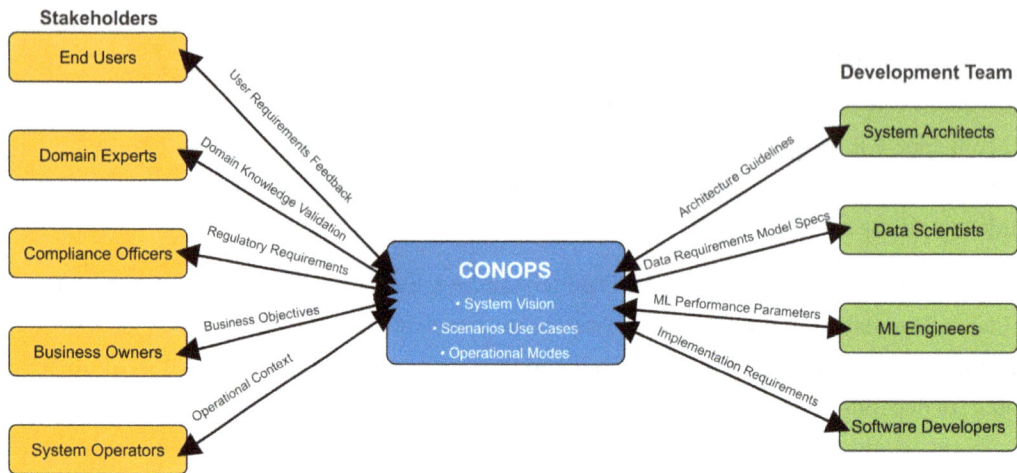

Figure 4.2: CONOPS stakeholder relationship diagram

As shown in *Figure 4.2*, the CONOPS document serves as a vital communication bridge connecting diverse stakeholders with development teams. On the left side, stakeholders, including end users, domain experts, compliance officers, business owners, and system operators, provide requirements and context. On the right side, development teams consisting of system architects, data scientists, ML engineers, and software developers receive specific guidance relevant to their roles. The central CONOPS document captures the system vision, scenarios, use cases, and operational modes, facilitating bidirectional information flow that ensures alignment and shared understanding.

CONOPS for AI-centric systems

For AI-centric systems, the CONOPS is where you first delineate how AI/ML technologies will create value. How will AI components increase revenue, lower costs, or transform operations? The functional components and processes that the AI system will impact must be clearly identified. AI aspects don't exist in isolation – their interfaces and coupled functionality need clear identification and understanding.

For modern AI systems, this means defining and understanding key data flows, including the following:

- Data ingestion pipelines and sources
- Data preprocessing and feature engineering requirements
- Model training, validation, and deployment workflows
- Inference processes and integration points
- Feedback loops for continuous learning

Control flow and execution processes must be captured to understand where and how AI components impact various system operation modes. IEEE 1362-2022 offers a good template for developing CONOPS documents for software-centric systems [1]. A thorough review of CONOPS is essential since many follow-on efforts flow from this set of artifacts.

Understanding the current system

To build a new system, start by understanding the current or prior system's limitations. A new system must add value beyond what currently exists – whether by increasing revenue, lowering costs, or improving other facets important to the end customer. Defining what will be built requires a description of the current system.

Items to highlight include the existing processes that bring value to current system stakeholders. You need to identify all stakeholders: users, customers, support personnel, business analysts, data scientists, compliance officers, and management levels. AI components invariably impact all stakeholders of the new system, so understanding how the current system affects these stakeholders is key to driving the new design. Identify metrics that show how the current system functions.

Data-centric view for AI systems

For AI-centric systems, data forms the heart of the system. At this phase, identify key data sources used in the current system. Focus on data filtering, transformations, or processing that supports the current system. Identify compliance or regulatory requirements to ensure the new AI-centric system meets them. The AI-centric system will likely need to replace, adapt, or create new functionality in this area.

Describe the current system's computational design and how it transforms data and arrives at inferences or control actions. Computational design encompasses processing, storage, and networking technologies along with associated performance specifications. In modern AI systems, this includes understanding the following:

- Current model architectures and their limitations
- Training and inference infrastructure
- Data storage and access patterns
- Latency requirements and bottlenecks
- Scaling capabilities and constraints
- DevOps and MLOps practices

Non-functional requirements for AI systems

AI-centric systems significantly drive the system's non-functional requirements. Non-functional requirements are typically satisfied using architectural tactics and patterns. The current system's architectural tactics and patterns must be understood to ensure the new AI-centric system replaces, adapts, or introduces new tactics and patterns consistently or better.

Understand the current system's limitations as much as possible. This aids in both gaining support for the new system and guiding other technical activities. Provide analysis and, if possible, empirical evidence supporting why the new system improves upon the system being replaced. The justification for change should describe opportunities not being realized or how the current system risks obsolescence from market competitors. For example, the extension of the Atlassian tool suites of Jira and Confluence added functionality for collaboration and integration. Though this was not a tremendous leap in added functionality. These systems are now industry-accepted and common usage tools. An older example of an AI technology was when Google changed their advertising pricing model where only if a link was executed was the client charged for advertising on Google. This simple CONOPS change significantly impacted Yahoo Inc.'s business model.

The business case for AI systems

A pointed question often asked about complex AI software is: "What is AI worth?"

Despite enthusiasm for applying AI technologies to increase profitability, ensuring the developed software system meets expectations requires clarifying where and how advantages will materialize. The complexity of software for AI-enabled systems needs to be managed so as to understand and mitigate the technical debt that accrues when needing to meet cost and time factors [2].

For a new system, first discuss and state what AI/ML technology will do for the organization [3]. How will AI/ML increase revenue, lower expenses, make the organization more efficient or safer, or improve other value metrics?

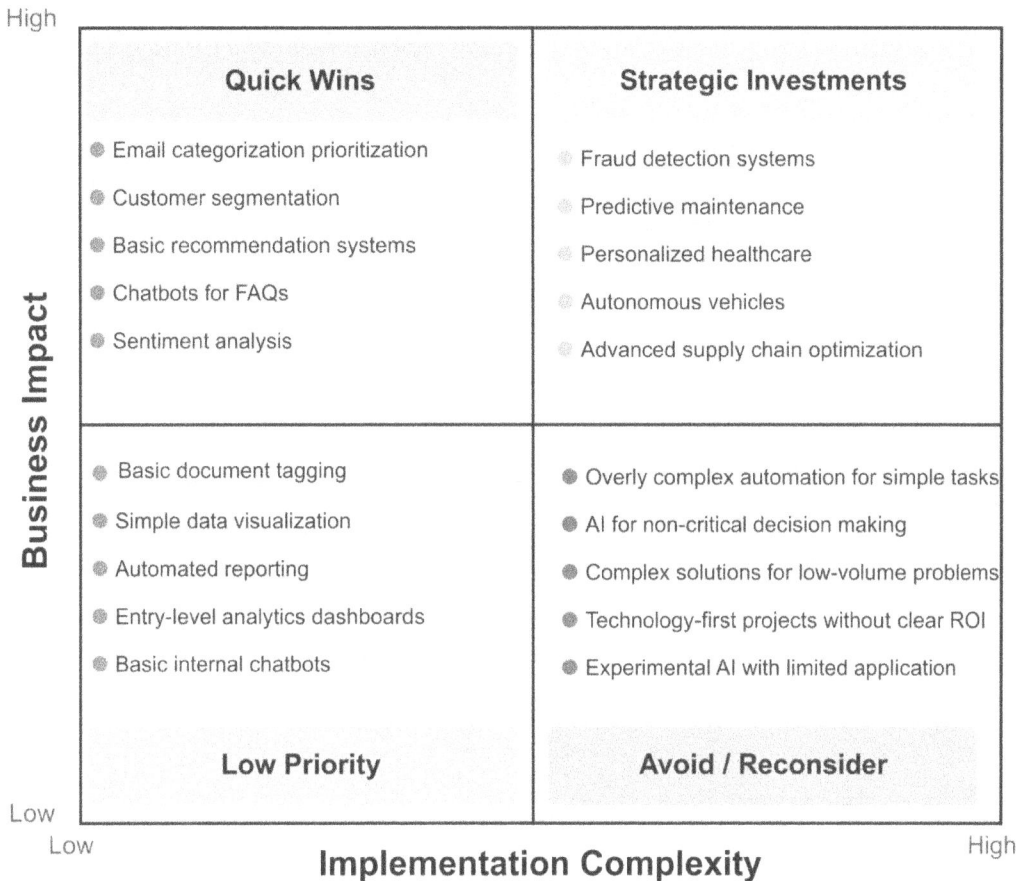

High

	Quick Wins	Strategic Investments

Quick Wins

- Email categorization prioritization
- Customer segmentation
- Basic recommendation systems
- Chatbots for FAQs
- Sentiment analysis

Strategic Investments

- Fraud detection systems
- Predictive maintenance
- Personalized healthcare
- Autonomous vehicles
- Advanced supply chain optimization

- Basic document tagging
- Simple data visualization
- Automated reporting
- Entry-level analytics dashboards
- Basic internal chatbots

- Overly complex automation for simple tasks
- AI for non-critical decision making
- Complex solutions for low-volume problems
- Technology-first projects without clear ROI
- Experimental AI with limited application

Low Priority

Avoid / Reconsider

Low

Low   **Implementation Complexity**   High

Business Impact

Figure 4.3: AI business value matrix

Figure 4.3 presents an AI business value matrix that helps organizations prioritize AI initiatives based on their implementation complexity and business impact. The matrix divides potential AI applications into four quadrants:

- **Quick wins (high impact, low complexity)**: Applications such as email categorization, customer segmentation, basic recommendation systems, chatbots for FAQs, and sentiment analysis offer significant business value with relatively straightforward implementation.

- **Strategic investments (high impact, high complexity)**: Projects such as fraud detection systems, predictive maintenance, personalized healthcare, autonomous vehicles, and advanced supply chain optimization require substantial resources but deliver high business value.

- **Low priority (low impact, low complexity)**: Basic functions such as document tagging, simple data visualization, automated reporting, entry-level analytics dashboards, and basic internal chatbots offer limited business impact despite being easy to implement.

- **Avoid/reconsider (low impact, high complexity)**: Projects such as overly complex automation for simple tasks, AI for non-critical decision-making, complex solutions for low-volume problems, technology-first projects without clear ROI, and experimental AI with limited application should be avoided or reconsidered.

This matrix provides a strategic framework for organizations to evaluate and prioritize their AI initiatives, ensuring resources are allocated to projects that balance technical feasibility with business value.

Impact of AI technologies on business operations

AI technologies impact the entire system from end to end. This systems perspective enables the evaluation of the technology's limits and what nominal operations or errors might impact the end system.

Understanding the performance metrics or requirements that the technology will affect – especially those impacting customer revenue or expenses – is crucial. Modern AI systems typically impact the following:

- Operational efficiency through automation

- Decision quality through advanced analytics

- Customer experience through personalization

- Risk management through predictive capabilities

- Resource allocation through optimization algorithms

- Speed to market through accelerated processes

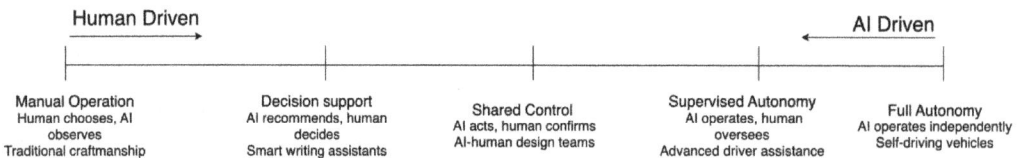

Figure 4.4: AI-human interaction spectrum

Figure 4.4 illustrates the AI-human interaction spectrum, showing the continuum from human-driven to AI-driven systems. This spectrum helps organizations conceptualize the intended level of autonomy and human involvement in their AI systems:

- **Manual operation**: Human chooses, AI observes (e.g., traditional craftsmanship)
- **Decision support**: AI recommends, human decides (e.g., smart writing assistants)
- **Shared control**: AI acts, human confirms (e.g., AI-human design teams)
- **Supervised autonomy**: AI operates, human oversees (e.g., advanced driver assistance)
- **Full autonomy**: AI operates independently (e.g., self-driving vehicles)

Understanding where your AI system falls on this spectrum is crucial for defining appropriate interaction models, establishing control protocols, and setting user expectations. It also helps in identifying potential risks and determining appropriate oversight mechanisms based on the level of AI autonomy.

Organizational integration and human impacts

The AI technology must fit within the organization's maintenance and development framework. Finally, delineate specific impacts on users and humans. AI technology invariably changes or adapts processes that humans conduct, including the following:

- Shifts in job roles from manual tasks to oversight functions
- Changes in decision-making authority and accountability
- New skill requirements for operation and maintenance
- Modified workflows and business processes
- Ethical considerations and transparency requirements
- Explainability needs for regulatory compliance [4]

Scenarios for AI-enabled systems

The right tool in the right context yields spectacular results – think of Michelangelo's chisel. Conversely, incorrectly used tools can bring disaster. Consider Zillow Corporation's massive losses exceeding $600 million due to the incorrect usage of AI models guiding their home-flipping business [6].

As part of conceptual design, sketch out the various roles and responsibilities of users. These roles span from external customers to system analysts, end users, system developers, and system operations and maintenance personnel. The AI technology's role and impact require architects to capture these viewpoints and accommodate them in the target baseline.

Creating effective scenarios

The roles document should explain how the system will accomplish its missions and tasks across relevant scenarios. Define an initial set of high-level metrics for both functional and non-functional requirements. Address key actors and how stakeholder concerns will be satisfied. Identify major architectural elements of the proposed system in the concept of operations.

Examples include determining whether the system will be centralized or distributed, identifying canonical actors, major external users or systems requiring integration, and any hard constraints such as regulatory or compliance requirements. Scenarios and use cases help with specifically understanding what the system must do and grounding follow-on engineering activities. Another important aspect is to conduct threat modeling scenarios to ensure the system is both secure and resilient in the face of adversarial and the full spectrum of cyber attacks.

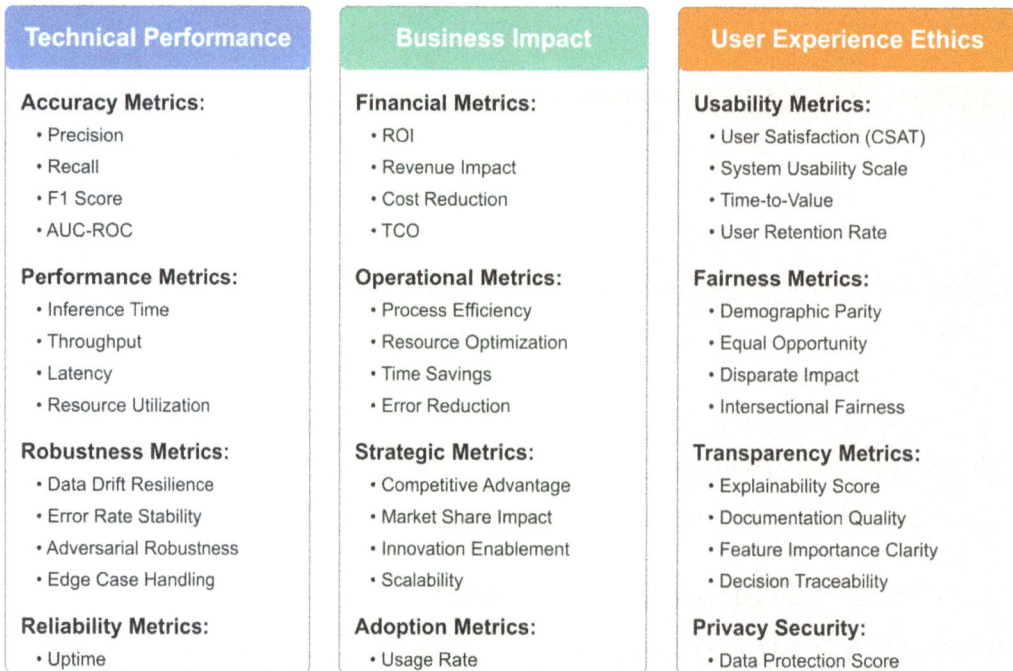

Technical Performance	Business Impact	User Experience Ethics
Accuracy Metrics:	**Financial Metrics:**	**Usability Metrics:**
• Precision	• ROI	• User Satisfaction (CSAT)
• Recall	• Revenue Impact	• System Usability Scale
• F1 Score	• Cost Reduction	• Time-to-Value
• AUC-ROC	• TCO	• User Retention Rate
Performance Metrics:	**Operational Metrics:**	**Fairness Metrics:**
• Inference Time	• Process Efficiency	• Demographic Parity
• Throughput	• Resource Optimization	• Equal Opportunity
• Latency	• Time Savings	• Disparate Impact
• Resource Utilization	• Error Reduction	• Intersectional Fairness
Robustness Metrics:	**Strategic Metrics:**	**Transparency Metrics:**
• Data Drift Resilience	• Competitive Advantage	• Explainability Score
• Error Rate Stability	• Market Share Impact	• Documentation Quality
• Adversarial Robustness	• Innovation Enablement	• Feature Importance Clarity
• Edge Case Handling	• Scalability	• Decision Traceability
Reliability Metrics:	**Adoption Metrics:**	**Privacy Security:**
• Uptime	• Usage Rate	• Data Protection Score

Figure 4.5: AI system success metrics framework

Figure 4.5 presents a comprehensive AI system success metrics framework that spans three essential domains:

- Technical performance:

  - Accuracy metrics: Precision, recall, F1 score, AUC-ROC

  - Performance metrics: Inference time, throughput, latency, resource utilization

  - Robustness metrics: Data drift resilience, error rate stability, adversarial robustness, edge case handling

  - Reliability metrics: Uptime

- Business impact:

  - Financial metrics: ROI, revenue impact, cost reduction, TCO

  - Operational metrics: Process efficiency, resource optimization, time savings, error reduction

  - Strategic metrics: Competitive advantage, market share impact, innovation enablement, scalability

  - Adoption metrics: Usage rate

- User experience and ethics:

  - Usability metrics: User satisfaction (CSAT), system usability scale, time to value, user retention rate

  - Fairness metrics: Demographic parity, equal opportunity, disparate impact, intersectional fairness

  - Transparency metrics: Explainability score, documentation quality, feature importance clarity, decision traceability

  - Privacy and security: Data protection score

This framework ensures that AI systems are evaluated holistically, beyond just technical accuracy, to include their business value and ethical implications. Scenarios should reference these metrics to define success criteria for the AI system.

AI technology usage in scenarios

In order to better understand the impacts of technology, there needs to be context. Scenarios are an excellent tool for defining context. Scenarios describe the challenges and major operation modes from a broader perspective. Take the following examples:

- How an AI-powered recommendation engine will personalize customer experiences
- How a predictive maintenance system will analyze sensor data to prevent equipment failures
- How a natural language processing system will handle customer service inquiries
- How a computer vision system will identify quality issues in manufacturing

A scenario might describe how a customer uses the system to make a purchase on an e-commerce website enhanced by AI-driven personalization. Or it may outline how medical professionals use the system for AI-assisted medical diagnosis. These scenarios should capture the major actors engaging with the system, identify key functions, and outline relevant metrics for evaluating system performance.

Defining success and constraints

Scenarios need to define what success means for the system, what constitutes nominal operation, and what would be failure conditions. Additionally, scenarios should describe technical constraints in more detail.

Examples of constraints might include accuracy requirements, acceptable false alarm probabilities, or maximum inference time limits. For modern AI systems, constraints might also include the following:

- Fairness and bias metrics for different demographic groups
- Explainability requirements for high-stakes decisions
- Data privacy and security standards
- Model drift thresholds triggering retraining
- Resource utilization limits during peak loads
- Fail-safe mechanisms when confidence thresholds aren't met

These scenarios don't need to be exhaustive but should be detailed enough that major stakeholders agree that the correct execution of these scenarios indicates successful system operation.

Use cases for AI-enabled systems

Use cases are very similar to scenarios in principle, but they are more detail-oriented so that they can guide actual software development. These diagrams capture interactions and more detailed functions to execute. Develop use cases hierarchically, where level 1 use cases collectively cover system execution per CONOPS. Derive lower-level use cases from level 1 use cases. Capture detailed human interactions for correct system operation and maintenance in the use cases.

Structure of effective use cases

Use cases should minimally include the following:

- Title
- Author
- System level and traceability
- Major actors
- Assumptions
- Pre-conditions
- Summary of execution
- Successful post-conditions
- Information output, warnings, alerts, alarms, and errors
- Post-conditions if the use case fails
- Data sources
- Data outputs

Use cases can clarify expected data sources, frequency, formats, and quality. At this stage in system architecture, very detailed use case decomposition isn't required – rather, focus on use cases highlighting the system's major nominal operational phases. As the design develops further, it should trace back to higher-level use cases. Use cases also help identify metrics and requirements for key system functionality, non-functional requirements, and system technical performance.

User classes and AI interaction

Formally define user classes at this stage. Identify how the AI component and all of the different human roles interact. Determine what data each role needs and how the AI supports that role. Define how interaction between the system and different roles will occur. Using an automation scale can help better explain how the AI component and human roles would be defined and built.

Operational modes for AI-enabled systems

The concepts of operations, scenarios, and use cases help define the system's major modes. For each mode, understand and document how AI-enabled components will work and what support they require across the rest of the system.

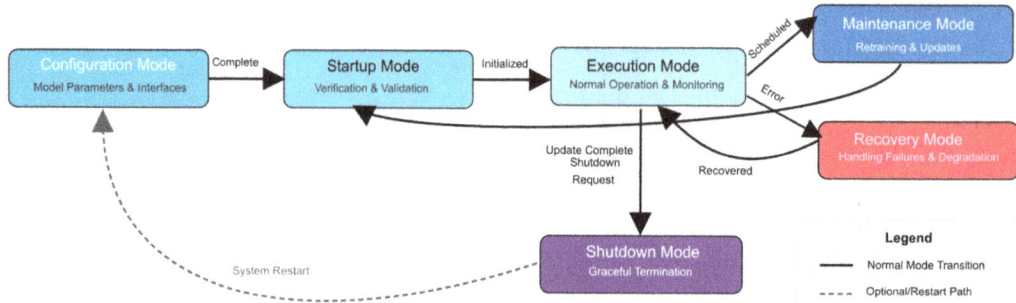

Figure 4.6: Six operational modes of AI systems and their transitions

Figure 4.6 illustrates the operational modes flowchart for AI systems, showing the six critical operational states and their transitions:

1. **Configuration mode**: Setting up model parameters and interfaces
2. **Startup mode**: Verification and validation of the system
3. **Execution mode**: Normal operation and monitoring
4. **Maintenance mode**: Retraining and updates
5. **Recovery mode**: Handling failures and degradation
6. **Shutdown mode**: Graceful termination

The diagram shows the normal flow path (solid lines) from configuration through startup to execution, with scheduled maintenance or error-triggered recovery paths. The dashed lines indicate optional restart paths. This operational modes framework is essential for comprehensive AI system planning, as it ensures all critical states are addressed in the system design.

Configuration mode

Identify needed model parameters and clarify mechanisms for the AI component to obtain them. Configure and ensure the readiness of external data interfaces, data sources, and human interface parameters. Provide logs or output confirming the AI component's readiness for startup. For modern AI systems, configuration includes the following:

- Model versioning and artifact management
- Feature stores and preprocessing pipelines
- A/B testing infrastructure
- Monitoring and observability setup
- Privacy-preserving mechanisms
- Hyper-parameter settings and optimization strategies

Startup mode

During startup, the AI-enabled component provides the integration status with the rest of the system. Run tests with known data and expected outputs to ensure proper AI component functioning. Log and positively communicate that the AI component and system are ready to execute. Modern practices include the following:

- Canary deployments to limit initial exposure
- Shadow mode operation alongside existing systems
- Progressive feature rollouts
- Automated validation against benchmark datasets
- Performance baseline measurements
- Infrastructure scaling verification

Execution mode

Collect statistics on system performance (typically machine learning metrics), operation counts, and pipeline health status, and capture warnings, alerts, alarms, or failures for reporting to users or system operators. Modern execution monitoring includes the following:

- Real-time model performance dashboards
- Drift detection and anomaly monitoring
- Feature importance tracking
- Resource utilization monitoring
- Serving latency and throughput metrics
- Data quality monitoring

Maintenance mode

Models typically require periodic maintenance based on classification or regression outputs due to expected model drift or obsolescence. Define how the AI component can be taken offline and how the rest of the pipeline(s) should perform without this component. Modern maintenance strategies include the following:

- Automated retraining pipelines triggered by performance degradation
- Champion-challenger model evaluation
- Continuous integration/continuous deployment for models
- Model governance and approval workflows
- Versioned datasets for reproducibility
- A/B testing frameworks for controlled rollouts

Recovery mode

After significant failure or off-nominal conditions, the AI component needs reconfiguration, testing, and preparation for redeployment to the production system. Depending on the recovery nature, model retraining may be necessary, requiring a cold standby strategy. Modern recovery approaches include the following:

- Model rollback capabilities
- Versioned model registry with quick-switch functionality
- Circuit breakers to fail gracefully to simpler models
- Ensembling techniques to reduce single-model dependence
- Cached inference results for critical paths
- Degraded mode operation plans

Shutdown mode

During shutdown, save the model and log operations to aid system restart. Implement fail-safe triggers so pipeline components aren't unduly impacted by AI component shutdown. Modern shutdown considerations include the following:

- Graceful handling of in-flight requests
- State preservation for stateful components
- Clean termination of resource-intensive processes
- Final telemetry capture for post-mortem analysis

- Coordinated shutdown sequencing with dependencies
- Proper release of cloud resources to control costs

Risk mitigation through conceptual design

The role of conceptual design also impacts the risk management for the overall system development. The conceptual design identifies the major scenario, associated use cases, requirements, and modeling to be accomplished. There is also the full gamut of AI technology evaluation and selection. This exercise then gives the system developers a holistic perspective of the system. This holistic view can then itself be decomposed and analyzed for various dimensions of risk that exist.

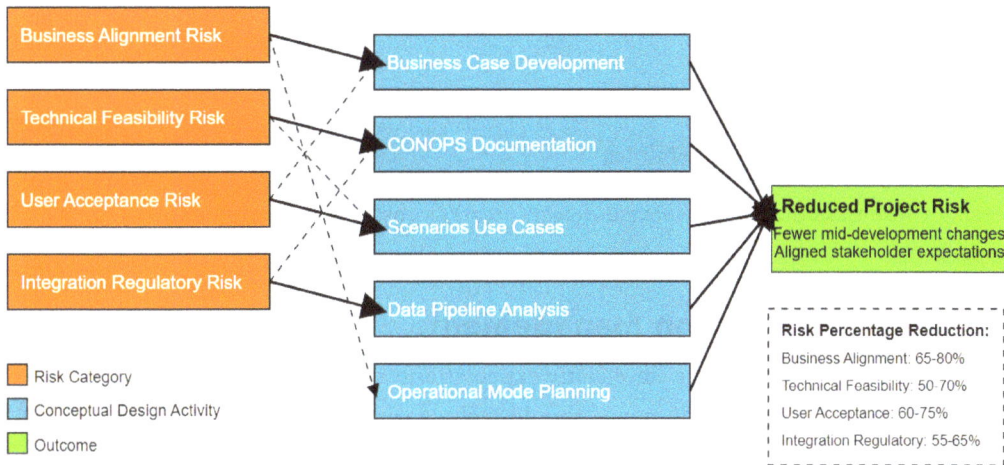

Figure 4.7: How conceptual design activities mitigate key risks in AI system development

Figure 4.7 illustrates how conceptual design activities directly address and mitigate key risks in AI system development. The diagram maps risk categories (orange) to specific conceptual design activities (blue) that address them, resulting in reduced project risk (green):

- Business alignment risk is mitigated through business case development (65–80% reduction)
- Technical feasibility risk is addressed through CONOPS documentation (50–70% reduction)
- User acceptance risk is reduced through scenarios and use cases (60–75% reduction)
- Integration and regulatory risk is mitigated through data pipeline analysis and operational mode planning (55–65% reduction)

The diagram shows how these activities collectively contribute to reduced project risk, resulting in fewer mid-development changes and better-aligned stakeholder expectations. This powerful visualization demonstrates the quantifiable value of thorough conceptual design in de-risking AI projects.

Data quality risk mitigation

AI systems are fundamentally dependent on data quality in ways traditional software is not. The CONOPS should include explicit data quality requirements and remediation strategies. Common data quality risks include the following:

- Incomplete or biased training data
- Inconsistent identifier tracking across systems
- Data drift over time
- Input data corruption or manipulation
- Privacy and security vulnerabilities

Addressing these risks during conceptual design prevents costly remediation efforts later in development.

Stakeholder expectation management

AI system stakeholders often have unrealistic expectations about model performance and capabilities. The conceptual design phase should include stakeholder education about the following:

- Realistic performance trajectories for AI systems
- The probabilistic nature of AI outputs
- The need for continuous monitoring and improvement
- Trade-offs between performance dimensions (accuracy versus explainability, etc.)
- The use of change management to ensure system stability and a record of changes

Setting appropriate expectations early prevents disappointment and project reassessment later.

Integration risk mitigation

AI systems rarely exist in isolation. They must integrate with legacy systems, data sources, and operational processes. Conceptual design should thoroughly address the following:

- Data compatibility across systems
- Latency requirements and constraints

- API specifications and contract definitions
- Fallback mechanisms when AI components underperform

Early consideration of integration challenges prevents costly architecture revisions during implementation. The NIST **AI Risk Management Framework (AI RMF)** is an excellent reference to aid in risk mitigation for the development of AI systems [5]. A tragic example of AI failure was the 2003 incident when a U.S. Patriot battery's autonomous software misidentified a U.K. fighter jet as a threat and shot the plane down, killing all pilots onboard.

Case study: Retail recommendation system

To illustrate the concepts discussed in this chapter, let's examine a real-world example of a retail recommendation system. A large e-commerce retailer wanted to improve their product recommendation system to increase customer engagement and sales.

CONOPS development

The CONOPS document defined how the AI recommendation system would integrate with existing e-commerce infrastructure, including the following:

- **Data sources**: Customer browsing history, purchase history, product catalog, and inventory systems
- **Performance expectations**: 50 ms recommendation generation latency, 15% increase in conversion rate
- **Constraints**: GDPR compliance, explainability for marketing teams

Business case

The business case quantified the expected benefits:

- 12% projected increase in average order value
- 8% reduction in cart abandonment
- Enhanced customer loyalty through personalization

Scenarios and use cases

Key scenarios included the following:

- Real-time recommendations during browsing
- Email campaign personalization
- Inventory-aware recommendations to prevent promoting out-of-stock items

Real-time recommendations during browsing was a chosen scenario since it forces design decisions on speed and model complexity. The email campaign personalization deals with the correct generation of names using natural language processing and other identifiers that demonstrate to customers that they are getting a specialized experience.

Inventory-aware recommendations force technical requirements to deal with up-to-date data stores, query complexity, analytic execution timing, and the system being able to respond to the situation of out-of-stock items.

Operational modes

The recommendation system required extensive configuration capabilities, including the following:

- Setting thresholds for similarity scores between products
- Configuring feature weights to balance recency, frequency, and monetary value
- Establishing integration parameters with inventory management systems
- Defining cold start strategies for new users and products

During normal operation, the system implemented the following:

- Real-time performance dashboards tracking recommendation relevance
- A/B testing infrastructure to continuously evaluate algorithm variants and hyper-parameters
- Automated alerts when conversion rates dropped below defined thresholds
- Session-based recommendation tracking to capture short-term intent

The system incorporated robust recovery mechanisms:

- Fallback to popularity-based recommendations if personalization failed
- Automatic switchover to pre-computed recommendations during traffic spikes
- Circuit breakers to isolate failing components without system-wide disruption
- Degraded operation modes that prioritized speed over personalization accuracy

Implementation challenges and lessons learned

In developing the recommendation system, the team discovered significant data quality issues in historical purchase records. Customer IDs were inconsistently tracked across platforms, creating challenges for building accurate user profiles. The conceptual design had to be revised to include more robust data cleaning pipelines and identity resolution mechanisms.

Marketing teams initially expected the recommendation engine to immediately achieve human-level personalization accuracy. The system architects had to educate stakeholders about realistic performance trajectories for AI systems, explaining how model accuracy improves over time with more data and feedback.

Integration with existing e-commerce infrastructure proved more complex than initially anticipated. Legacy inventory systems had significantly different data models and update latencies than required for real-time recommendations. The team revised their architectural approach to include an intermediate data synchronization layer that decoupled the recommendation service from legacy systems.

Summary

In this chapter, we've explored the critical importance of conceptual design for AI-enabled systems. The conceptual design phase establishes the foundation upon which all subsequent engineering activities build. For AI-enabled systems, this foundation is particularly crucial due to their unique characteristics: data dependencies, learning behavior, probabilistic outcomes, and human-AI interaction complexities.

Key takeaways include the following:

- Understanding how the proposed system will bring value to end customers
- Understanding what AI/ML will provide to the new system
- Identifying what the new system must do, what would be helpful to do, and what the new system cannot do
- Identifying performance and non-functional requirements from the customer's perspective
- Documenting insights in a concept of operations tailored to customers and stakeholders, and accessible to a general audience
- Identifying key roles, actors, and use cases for the end-to-end system, highlighting where AI/ML components are prominent

When properly executed, conceptual design mitigates the most significant risk in AI system development: building the wrong system. By investing adequate resources in this phase, organizations dramatically increase the likelihood of delivering AI systems that satisfy user needs, fulfill business objectives, and operate safely and effectively within their intended context.

This chapter's content was necessarily broad because each software system, context, and customer is unique. A common thread in architecting is that conceptual design mitigates many risks. The resulting artifacts form the foundation for follow-on engineering activities, which is especially critical for AI-enabled systems where the cost of misalignment can be substantial.

The next chapters will build upon this foundation, exploring how the conceptual design artifacts guide the development of detailed requirements, architectural design decisions, and implementation strategies for AI-enabled systems.

Exercises

1. **AI business value matrix application**

   Consider an industry you're familiar with (healthcare, retail, manufacturing, etc.). Identify four potential AI applications for this industry, placing one in each quadrant of the AI business value matrix (quick win, strategic investment, low priority, avoid/reconsider). Justify your placement decisions based on implementation complexity and business impact factors.

2. **Scenario development for AI-human interaction**

   Create a detailed scenario for an AI system that falls in the "Shared Control" portion of the AI-human interaction spectrum. Your scenario should describe the context, primary actors, AI component responsibilities, human operator responsibilities, and key interaction points. Include potential failure modes and how they would be handled.

3. **Use case specification**

   Write a complete use case for a maintenance mode operation in an AI-enabled predictive maintenance system. Follow the structure outlined in the *Structure of effective use cases* section, ensuring you include all 12 required elements. Pay particular attention to pre-conditions, post-conditions, and error-handling mechanisms.

4. **Risk mitigation planning**

   For an AI-enabled medical diagnosis assistant system, identify three specific risks in each of the following categories: data quality risks, stakeholder expectation risks, and integration risks. For each risk, describe how you would address it during the conceptual design phase to prevent issues during implementation.

References

1. IEEE Computer Society. (2022). IEEE 1362-2022: IEEE Guide for Information Technology - System Definition - **Concept of Operatio**ns (ConOps) Document. IEEE Standards Association. DOI: 10.1109/IEEESTD.2022.9767507

2. Sculley, D., Holt, G., Golovin, D., Davydov, E., Phillips, T., Ebner, D., Chaudhary, V., Young, M., Crespo, J. F., & Dennison, D. (2015). Hidden Technical Debt in Machine Learning Systems. Advances in Neural Information Processing Systems, 28, 2503-2511. `https://papers. nips.cc/paper/2015/hash/86df7dcfd896fcaf2674f757a2463eba-Abstract.html`

3. Amershi, S., Begel, A., Bird, C., DeLine, R., Gall, H., Kamar, E., Nagappan, N., Nushi, B., & Zimmermann, T. (2019). Software Engineering for Machine Learning: A Case Study. IEEE/ACM 41st International Conference on Software Engineering: Software Engineering in Practice (ICSE-SEIP), 291-300. DOI: 10.1109/ICSE-SEIP.2019.00042

4. Arrieta, A. B., Díaz-Rodríguez, N., Del Ser, J., Bennetot, A., Tabik, S., Barbado, A., García, S., Gil-López, S., Molina, D., Benjamins, R., Chatila, R., & Herrera, F. (2020). **Explainable Artificial Intelligence** (**XAI**): Concepts, taxonomies, opportunities and challenges toward responsible AI. Information Fusion, 58, 82-115. DOI: 10.1016/j.inffus.2019.12.012

5. National Institute of Standards and Technology. (2022). Artificial Intelligence Risk Management Framework (AI RMF 1.0). U.S. Department of Commerce. `https://doi. org/10.6028/NIST.AI.100-1`

6. "Zillow iBuying: What Happened", Robust Intelligence, Perspectives November 16, 2021, `https://www.robustintelligence.com/blog-posts/zillows-ibuying-failures`

5

Requirements and Architecture for AI Pipelines

Machine learning model development fundamentally differs from traditional software engineering in its experimental and iterative nature. While software engineers typically design systems based on well-defined specifications, data scientists must navigate the inherent uncertainties of data characteristics, feature relevance, and model behavior. This necessitates a systematic yet flexible approach to model creation, optimization, and validation that accommodates the unique challenges of AI development.

This chapter examines "AI pipeline systems" – the predominant architecture in enterprise AI today, which consist of progressive processing stages utilizing interconnected AI models. These pipelines form the backbone of modern AI implementations, enabling organizations to systematically develop, deploy, and maintain AI capabilities at scale.

AI systems rarely operate as standalone modules; rather, they are typically embedded within larger software ecosystems and follow structured development and deployment workflows. This chapter thoroughly examines the architecture and requirements of both development and production pipelines, with particular emphasis on the critical process of transitioning models from experimental environments into robust production systems [1][2].

This chapter will provide comprehensive guidance on the following:

- The major facets required for creating effective development and production pipelines
- How to leverage modular architecture to improve AI system performance and meet crucial non-functional requirements
- Essential architecture tactics and patterns specifically designed for AI-enabled systems

Development pipelines

Architecture emerges from requirements, creating a recursive pattern where components synthesized from initial requirements themselves become requirements for subsequent architectural synthesis. This recursion continues until system builders can no longer meaningfully impact associated sub-components, at which point implementation details take precedence.

A robust development environment serves as the foundation for testing and validating pipelines before production release. Comprehensive architecture models identify major components, external interfaces, user involvement points, and data requirements throughout the system. Multiple architecture views capture process flows and operational threads, demonstrating how AI systems will systematically meet both explicit and implicit requirements [3].

Modular design significantly enhances system flexibility and maintainability, particularly in complex AI pipelines. Each stage in an AI pipeline should be independently verifiable, configurable, and scalable to accommodate changing requirements and technological advances. The pipeline needs to be versioned and have clear traceability to its data lineage. The architecture must capture both functional components and non-functional requirements such as scalability, reliability, and observability, creating a holistic blueprint for implementation.

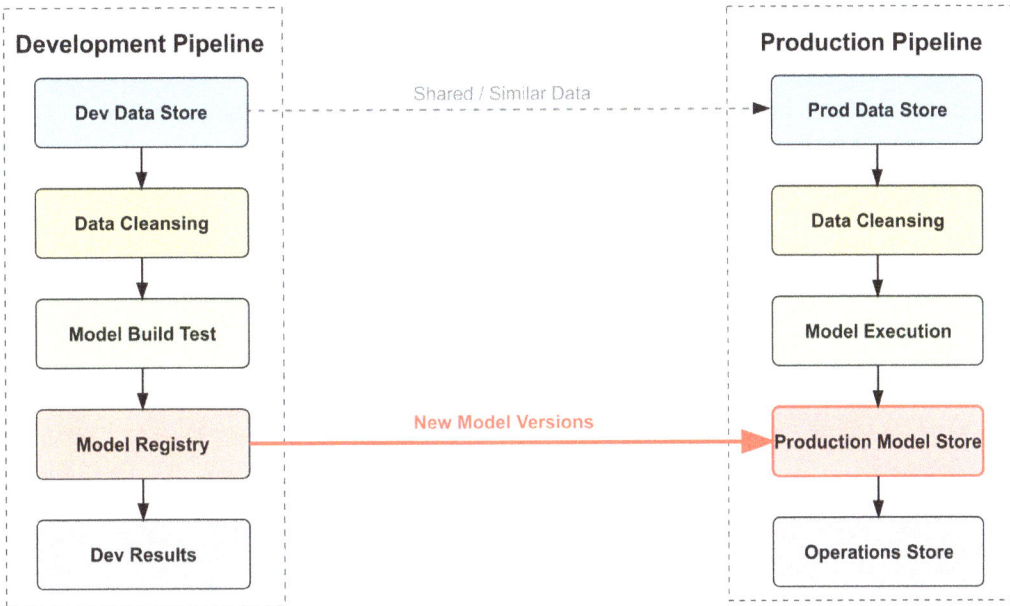

Figure 5.1: High-level AI pipeline overview

In *Figure 5.1*, we see the relationship between development and production pipelines in an AI system illustrated. The left side depicts the development pipeline where model building and experimentation occur, while the right side shows the production pipeline where operational model deployment and inference take place. This visual representation highlights the parallel nature of these environments and their critical interconnections.

The development pipeline consists of several key components working in concert:

- The **Dev Data Store** serves as a repository for training and testing data
- **Data Cleansing** processes ensure data quality and consistency
- The **Model Build Test** environment provides infrastructure for model training and evaluation
- The **Model Registry** enables versioning and tracking of models, including the parameters used in models
- **Dev Results** repositories store development outcomes for analysis and comparison

The production pipeline mirrors this structure with components designed for operational use:

- The **Prod Data Store** maintains operational data
- Similar **Data Cleansing** processes ensure production data quality

- **Model Execution** provides the infrastructure where inference occurs
- The **Production Model Store** securely houses deployed models
- **Operations Store** components enable comprehensive monitoring and management

The central arrow in *Figure 5.1* demonstrates how models, once thoroughly validated, transition from development to production environments. The two pipelines share similar data structures and processing approaches (shown by the top connection) to ensure that production deployment conditions closely resemble development environments, reducing the risk of unexpected behavior when models go live.

These architectural views feed directly into systems analysis activities, identifying which parts need detailed modeling to drive design decisions and provide initial evaluation of expected performance metrics. They also help identify specific metrics and data requirements across all AI system components, ensuring comprehensive coverage of both functional and non-functional requirements.

With a clearly specified architecture in place, work can be effectively allocated for implementation. Teams typically organize along the system architecture boundaries, using configuration-controlled diagrams to communicate the overarching vision, facilitate cross-team communication, and efficiently onboard new team members as the project evolves.

AI-enabled systems require holistic requirements engineering, as AI components never exist in isolation but rather operate within complex technological ecosystems. Requirements must comprehensively specify data engineering aspects, computational hardware needs, and precisely how the broader system will ingest and act upon AI-generated decisions.

Data store requirements

The data store serves as the pipeline's foundation and source of truth, typically incorporating minimal processing to maintain data integrity. Several key considerations must be addressed when designing this critical component.

Data volume and velocity

Understanding the total volume of data expected for processing is essential for proper infrastructure planning. This includes projections for data growth over time and peak processing requirements. Similarly, data velocity requirements into stores must be clearly specified, including patterns of data flow and expected variability throughout operational cycles.

Data formats and processing approaches

Requirements must address both structured and unstructured data types, including specifications for standardization and compatibility. Processing-type decisions – whether batch processing, streaming, or hybrid approaches – significantly impact architecture and should be driven by system goals and performance requirements.

Timeliness and technology selection

Processing speed requirements and acceptable delays must be explicitly defined based on business needs. Data store technology selection – whether relational databases, object stores, graph databases, or specialized AI data stores – should be guided by system goals and performance requirements rather than technological preferences.

Non-functional requirements and governance

Storage redundancy, replication strategies, and backup frequency must be established based on data criticality and recovery objectives. Security protocols, governance frameworks, and compliance requirements play crucial roles in mitigating risks and ensuring regulatory adherence, particularly for sensitive data.

Support operations and specialized stores

Status information, monitoring capabilities, and alerting systems must be built into the data architecture to enable proactive management. Modern AI systems increasingly leverage specialized data stores, including vector databases for similarity searches, feature stores for consistent transformations, and lakehouses that combine data lake flexibility with data warehouse structure.

Storage technology	Domain considerations	Compliance
Relational	High consistency Performance Structured data	Data provenance Up-to-date records
Object	Unstructured data Speed of storage Minimal indexing Flexible data schemas	Maintenance Records of full data volumes

Key-Value	Flexible schema	Fast recovery of data
	Need for rapid query search	Records of full data volumes
Graph	Speed of lookup	Data provenance
	Simple data model	Fast data summaries
	Can mimic domain	
Vector	Natural language processing	Data associations
	Large language models	Proof of training datasets

Table 5.1: Comparison of data storage technologies

Algorithmic development components

As has been stated, the building of an AI system has as its core the building of components that are expected to make decisions. The decisions that are to be made rely heavily or almost entirely on the data that comes into the system. A decision is only as good and valid as the data that was used. The next sections describe key tasks that can be used to ensure the highest quality of data enters the system. These tasks can be both tedious and challenging since, for the initial system development, a human is needed. That said, for further system development, these tasks can be done in an automated manner with checking and alerting.

Data quality checks

Understanding data quality is critical for effectively training, tuning, and maintaining AI pipelines. Quality checks should be rigorously configuration-controlled and tested, with minimum requirements explicitly specified. These include comprehensive assessments of data completeness to ensure records have values for all required fields, corruption detection to identify malformed data, time-span regularity verification to maintain temporal consistency, format validation to confirm expected data structures, and range checking to verify field values remain within expected boundaries.

Modern quality control approaches also incorporate automated validation for detecting data drift and anomalies as they emerge, along with sophisticated bias testing methodologies to proactively identify and mitigate potential biases before they affect model performance. These mechanisms form an essential foundation for maintaining data integrity throughout the AI pipeline lifecycle.

Data transforms

Pipeline data rarely arrives in formats directly usable by machine learning models. Data transforms normalize and prepare data for inference, and their implementation must be thoroughly understood, precisely formulated, and rigorously checked. Common transformations include converting between different geographic data formats, standardizing physical units for consistent representation, applying dimensionality reduction techniques to improve model efficiency, and implementing feature stores to ensure transformation consistency across development and production environments.

Advanced transformation approaches incorporate representation learning to automatically discover useful data representations and data augmentation strategies to artificially expand training datasets. These transformations must be treated as first-class citizens in the pipeline architecture, with appropriate version control and monitoring to ensure consistency.

Data summary

Data summaries serve dual purposes: verifying model consistency and supporting ongoing pipeline monitoring. Effective summaries include comprehensive dataset statistics (mean, median, variability metrics), data field association analysis to identify relationships, distribution fitting to understand underlying patterns, and visual representations through techniques such as box plots and interactive dashboards.

Modern approaches incorporate anomaly detection in distributions to identify potential data quality issues and correlation analysis to understand feature relationships. These summaries provide critical visibility into data characteristics that impact model performance and should be maintained throughout the pipeline lifecycle.

Model building, tuning, and verification

Model building should be conceptualized as an ongoing iterative process rather than a terminal task, since AI pipelines must continuously adapt to evolving data patterns and business requirements. The pipeline architecture must support reproducible training, systematic tuning, and rigorous evaluation to ensure consistent performance over time.

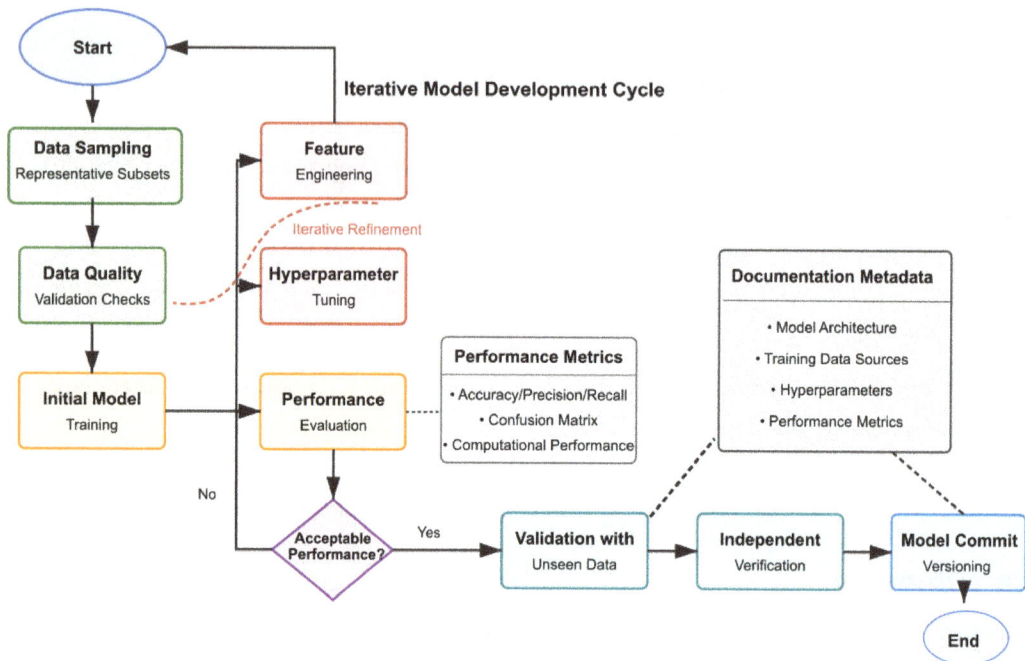

Figure 5.2: Model building, tuning, and verification workflow

In *Figure 5.2*, we see the iterative nature of model development illustrated from initial data sampling through deployment. The workflow begins with data sampling to create representative subsets, followed by data quality validation, initial model training, and performance evaluation against established metrics. The workflow then reaches a critical decision point: Is the performance acceptable based on predefined criteria? If not, the process loops back for refinement through feature engineering to optimize model inputs and hyperparameter tuning to adjust model configuration.

Once performance reaches acceptable thresholds, the model proceeds through validation with unseen data to test generalizability, independent verification by someone not involved in development to reduce bias, and formal model commit procedures to version the final model for deployment. Throughout this process, comprehensive documentation metadata is maintained, including model architecture details, training data sources, hyperparameter settings, and performance metrics.

Several key infrastructure considerations support this workflow:

Configuration control

Successful AI pipelines require disciplined tracking throughout their lifecycle, including time-phasing and temporal tagging of datasets, comprehensive metadata reference and activity logging, and robust model registries for versioning. Modern implementations leverage experiment tracking platforms using tools such as Git, MLflow, or DVC to maintain complete traceability of the development process.

Machine learning performance

Effective pipelines require a clear understanding of expected outputs and processing times, comprehensive performance metrics (confusion matrices, accuracy, AUC), visualization tools for comparing results to expectations, and multi-metric evaluation approaches that consider fairness and explainability alongside traditional performance measures. Ongoing monitoring for model drift is essential for maintaining performance over time.

Computation infrastructure

Pipeline design must include thorough testing on the target computing infrastructure to ensure performance requirements are met, benchmarking storage and network impact to identify potential bottlenecks, and implementing model optimization techniques such as quantization and pruning where appropriate. Modern implementations often incorporate hardware acceleration and inference optimization to maximize efficiency.

Scale processing

Enterprise-grade pipelines require infrastructure for testing models at production scale, comprehensive load testing with production-level traffic patterns, shadow deployment capabilities to run new models alongside existing systems, and chaos engineering approaches to verify system resilience under adverse conditions.

Model tuning and verification

Models typically require systematic fine-tuning to address end-to-end system requirements beyond initial performance metrics. Comprehensive verification should include second checks comparing test data to production samples to verify consistency, independent review by someone not involved in development to reduce bias, result visualization to identify potential outliers, and interface checks to ensure compatibility with downstream systems.

Advanced approaches incorporate hyperparameter optimization techniques to maximize performance, adversarial testing methodologies to identify potential weaknesses, red teaming processes, and explainable AI techniques to enhance model transparency. These verification processes ensure models will perform reliably when deployed to production environments.

Code committal and DevOps

The final development step involves integrating the validated model into the pre-production baseline. This code will be used for comprehensive testing and staging, with representative data samples and production data utilized to identify potential integration impacts before full deployment.

Modern approaches to this stage include automated CI/CD pipelines specifically designed for ML workflows, containerization technologies for consistent deployment across environments, infrastructure-as-code practices for reproducibility, feature flags for controlled functionality rollout, and blue-green deployment strategies for minimizing disruption during transitions.

Production pipeline

The production pipeline represents the culmination of extensive development work and stakeholder expectations – the operational "kitchen" that must consistently deliver on promises made during planning and development. This section provides detailed guidance on production pipeline architecture and technical requirements.

Data stores

Many pipeline issues can be traced back to misunderstood requirements or implementation decisions around data stores. Engineering efforts should begin by carefully considering the expected output characteristics: speed requirements, quality thresholds, timing constraints, and intended recipients.

Data store technology considerations include several options with distinct strengths and limitations.

Relational data stores excel with stable data models and minimal scalability concerns, providing strong consistency guarantees and transaction support. Object stores handle diverse components that don't fit standard schemas, enabling easy attribute modification and rapid horizontal scaling at the cost of some consistency guarantees. Document stores combine object store flexibility with schema structure, providing a middle ground for semi-structured data. Graph stores leverage mathematical graph structures for data relationships, delivering exceptional latency performance for graph-centric analytics and relationship queries.

Log stores process data as immutable event streams with minimal processing, shifting analytical burden to downstream pipeline components while providing strong auditability. Modern specialized stores such as vector databases, feature stores, and time-series databases offer purpose-built capabilities for specific AI workloads, often delivering substantial performance improvements for their target use cases.

Data operations

Data stores must consistently meet pipeline performance requirements through several key operational capabilities.

Comprehensive benchmarking of data rates and operations ensures infrastructure can handle expected workloads under various conditions. Flexible architecture with robust reporting enables adaptation to changing requirements while maintaining visibility. Data quality monitoring systems proactively identify potential issues before they impact downstream processes. Automated and semi-automated schema evolution capabilities allow systems to adapt to changing data structures without disruption. If using automated schema changes, it is imperative that there are architectural-level safeguards such as alerts, archives, and versioning to prevent data loss. Data lineage tracking provides complete visibility into how data flows through complex pipeline systems.

Data cleansing

This stage meticulously prepares data to ensure correct model execution in production environments. Key aspects include integrity checks to verify data isn't garbled or incomplete during transmission, format checks to ensure values match expected encoding and format specifications, and consistency checks that implement domain-driven semantic validation for logical validity.

Data cleansing serves as an essential quality gate for building confidence in pipeline outputs, though it has inherent limitations – it's practically impossible to check for all potential issues within complex data streams. Well-designed cleansing processes focus on high-impact validations based on domain knowledge and historical error patterns.

Data transformation

This final preprocessing step before model execution normalizes data across various dimensions, including timestamps, geographical references, terminology standards, and numeric ranges. These transformations should be thoroughly tested and validated to prevent subtle errors from propagating through to model execution.

Modern approaches to transformation include feature stores for maintaining consistency across environments, transfer learning techniques for generating robust representations, neural network-based transformations for complex pattern extraction, and automated feature engineering to discover optimal representations.

Model execution

In production environments, model execution should be treated as a carefully managed black box without direct updates during operation. Key operational aspects include the following.

Operational status monitoring

Production pipelines require comprehensive metrics collection on data flows, processing times, and hardware performance to maintain visibility. This status information should be presented through multiple complementary channels: visual dashboards for at-a-glance assessment, detailed graphs and plots for trend analysis, key performance indicators, log output summaries for troubleshooting, and real-time alerts for performance issues requiring immediate attention.

Production Pipeline

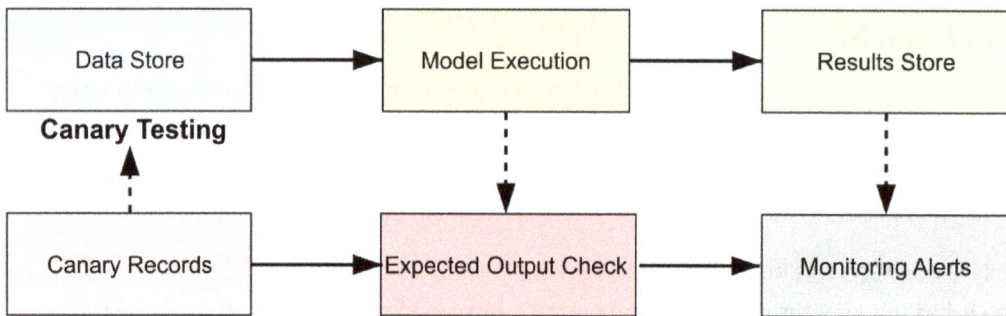

Figure 5.3: Production inference execution canary checks

🔍 **Quick tip**: Need to see a high-resolution version of this image? Open this book in the next-gen Packt Reader or view it in the PDF/ePub copy.

📖 **The next-gen Packt Reader** and a **free PDF/ePub copy** of this book are included with your purchase. Scan the QR code OR visit `https://packtpub.com/unlock`, then use the search bar to find this book by name. Double-check the edition shown to make sure you get the right one.

In *Figure 5.3*, we see how canary testing is implemented in production pipelines to monitor model health. The diagram illustrates the standard production pipeline flow from **Data Store** through **Model Execution** to **Results Store** in the top row, with the canary testing infrastructure shown in the bottom row. This infrastructure includes carefully curated canary records containing known inputs with expected outputs, expected output check components that compare actual model outputs to expected results, and monitoring alerts that trigger notifications when deviations exceed threshold values.

This canary data provides a continuous stream of validation, with known inputs and expected outputs verifying ongoing model health. Deviations from expected results trigger alerts, indicating potential model drift or pipeline issues requiring investigation. This early warning system helps maintain model reliability in production environments by identifying problems before they significantly impact business operations.

Implementing these canary checks is essential for detecting subtle model drift over time, identifying infrastructure issues affecting model performance, building stakeholder confidence in ongoing model operations, and providing a mechanism for controlled testing in production environments without disrupting normal operations.

Model maintenance

Continuous monitoring processes determine when model redeployment is warranted based on changing datasets, performance degradation, or shifting business requirements. These processes should balance the need for model stability against the benefits of incorporating new data and refinements.

Results and end user stores

These components collect model outputs and associated metadata, serving as interfaces for downstream systems and human users. They should provide powerful querying mechanisms for flexible data access, enable machine-to-machine data ingestion through standardized APIs, support comprehensive visualization capabilities, maintain traceability between inputs and outputs, generate appropriate explanations for non-technical users, and integrate seamlessly with business intelligence platforms.

Pipeline operations store

This component focuses on overall control and maintenance of the pipeline ecosystem, providing several critical capabilities.

Human operation inputs enable authorized interventions when necessary, supported by a robust alerting framework that prioritizes notifications based on severity and impact. Operations data collection centralizes pipeline telemetry for analysis, with pipeline logging visualization tools converting complex data into actionable insights. Modern implementations include sophisticated incident response systems for managing disruptions and comprehensive compliance documentation to satisfy regulatory requirements.

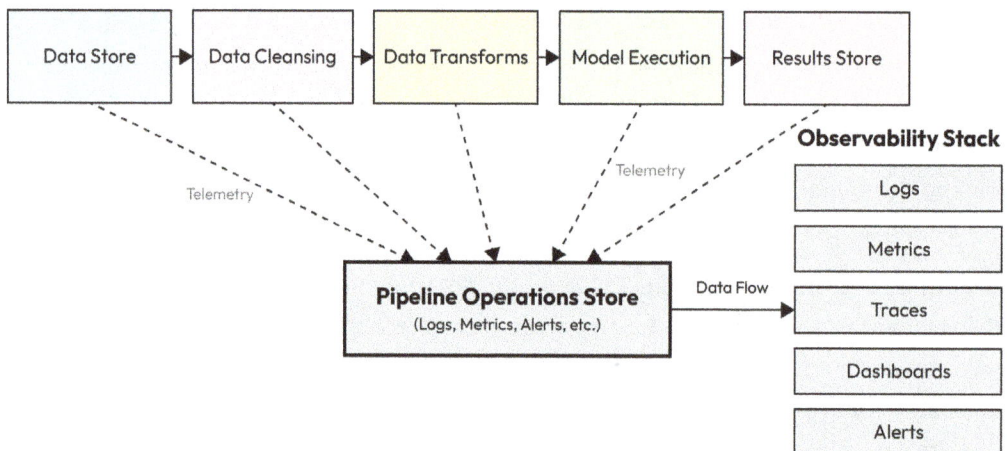

Figure 5.4: Pipeline operations store observability

In *Figure 5.4*, we see the observability architecture for AI pipelines illustrated. The diagram shows the main pipeline components (**Data Store**, **Data Cleansing**, **Data Transforms**, **Model Execution**, and **Results Store**) in the top row, with each component sending telemetry data to the central **Pipeline Operations Store**. This centralized repository collects logs, metrics, alerts, and other operational data, feeding into the comprehensive **Observability Stack** shown on the right side.

This architecture enables sophisticated performance correlation analysis across pipeline components, allowing operators to identify processing bottlenecks, track data flow through all system components, monitor system health in real time, troubleshoot issues with comprehensive visibility, and analyze historical performance trends to guide optimization efforts.

A robust operations store serves as the nervous system of the AI pipeline, essential for both reactive troubleshooting when issues arise and proactive performance optimization to prevent problems before they impact operations.

Continuous development/integration

DevOps methodologies enable rapid pipeline prototyping and testing without disrupting production operations. The "Blue and Gold" deployment concept works particularly well in AI contexts:

1. One pipeline operates in production while another is built in parallel.
2. When ready, the test pipeline connects to production data for comparative evaluation.
3. If performance is satisfactory, it seamlessly becomes the new production pipeline.

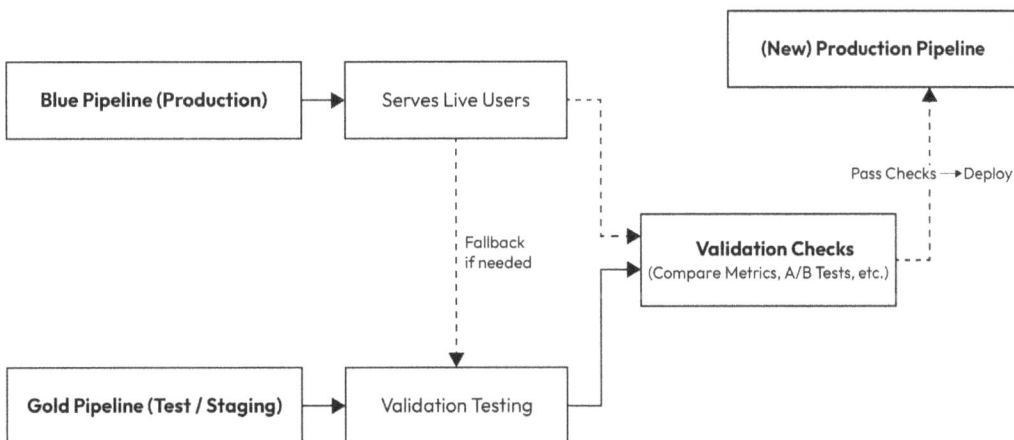

Figure 5.5: CI/CD for AI pipelines – "Blue and Gold" deployment

In *Figure 5.5*, we see the "Blue and Gold" deployment strategy for AI pipelines illustrated. The diagram shows the current production pipeline (**Blue**) serving live users, while the test/staging pipeline (**Gold**) with new models or updates undergoes validation testing. Comprehensive validation checks compare metrics, A/B test results, and other performance indicators between the two environments.

The workflow follows a specific process where code changes trigger CI/CD pipelines, the "Gold" environment executes the new model version, validation checks compare performance between Blue and Gold implementations, and if successful, Gold transitions to production status while the previous production pipeline remains available as a fallback for immediate rollback if needed.

This approach ensures safe testing of new models without disrupting production operations, direct comparison between current and new implementations under identical conditions, controlled transition to production when quality thresholds are verified, and straightforward rollback mechanisms if issues are discovered after deployment.

Modern MLOps practices extend these capabilities with experiment tracking to maintain development history, model registries for version control, feature stores for transformation consistency, automated testing frameworks for quality assurance, and continuous training pipelines that automatically incorporate new data.

Architecture patterns and tactics

Architecture extends far beyond functional descriptions to address crucial non-functional requirements that determine real-world system success. Software tactics (first-order methods solving specific problems) and patterns (strategic combinations of tactics addressing complex problems) serve as foundational building blocks for complex systems.

Several architectural patterns specifically support AI pipeline development:

- Pipe and filter architecture enables sequential and parallel processing where each stage transforms data and passes it downstream, creating a clear separation of concerns and facilitating independent scaling
- Distributed store approaches spread data across multiple systems to improve performance, resilience, and scalability beyond single-node limitations
- Blackboard architecture creates a shared repository for intermediate artifacts with pull-based components, enabling flexible processing workflows and simplified component interactions
- Service orientation encapsulates functionality into weakly-coupled services communicating via well-defined APIs, improving maintainability and enabling independent evolution of components

Key tactics employed within these patterns include the following:

- Ping-echo mechanisms enable components to query others for responses, verifying connectivity and basic functionality

- Heartbeat monitoring establishes regular signals indicating continued operation and pipeline health, providing early warning of component failures

- N-party voting implements consensus mechanisms where multiple entities vote on actions, improving decision reliability in uncertain contexts

- Canary testing systematically identifies model drift or errors before full deployment by comparing results against known-good references

- Versioned models and datasets enable comprehensive rollback capabilities and traceability throughout the system lifecycle

Non-functional requirements

A key concept is that architecture considerations for a software system are driven by the non-functional requirements. There exist dozens of non-functional requirements. The role of the architect is to understand the client's needs, the business case, and technical dimensions to formulate what are the key non-functional requirements for that given system. The non-functional requirements that are discussed next are major ones that usually surface across systems. You should not construe these as the only ones, that all these must be used, or that others cannot be identified.

Reliability

AI pipelines must ensure system availability when needed through several mechanisms: error containment to prevent cascading failures, robust messaging infrastructure resistant to transient failures, redundancy and rollback mechanisms for quick recovery, chaos engineering practices to verify resilience, and automated incident response to minimize human intervention requirements.

Maintainability

Support for ongoing model development and updates requires careful architectural decisions: technology minimization to reduce complexity, well-defined interfaces between components, microservices architecture for independent evolution, and infrastructure-as-code practices to ensure reproducibility across environments.

Usability

Effective pipelines provide consistent configuration methods across components, robust logging with centralized information access, clear version control for all artifacts, intuitive graphical interfaces for monitoring and management, and self-service platforms enabling data scientists to operate independently within governed frameworks.

Summary

Architecting AI pipelines requires careful coordination between data management, model development, infrastructure design, and software integration practices. The comprehensive pipeline architecture involves parallel development pipelines (for model creation and testing) and production pipelines (for deployment and value delivery), connected through well-defined transition processes.

Key considerations for successful implementation include data-centric design focusing on stores with appropriate characteristics for specific workloads, modular architecture with well-defined and independently verifiable components, quality assurance through comprehensive data checks and transformations, monitoring and observability across all pipeline components, DevOps integration enabling rapid iteration and controlled deployment, non-functional requirements driving architectural decisions beyond basic functionality, and governance and compliance frameworks embedded throughout both pipeline environments.

A successful pipeline must satisfy not only the functional requirements of AI model training and inference but also the non-functional demands of scalability, observability, and governance that determine real-world operational success. Modern AI systems increasingly adopt MLOps practices that balance innovation and flexibility with production stability, creating sustainable frameworks for ongoing development.

The architecture must ultimately support technical excellence, business value delivery, user adoption, and responsible AI practices – a multifaceted challenge requiring both technical expertise and strategic vision to navigate successfully. With much of the conceptual design of the system in place, we will now shift to discuss the key steps to get to an implementation. In the next chapter, we will discuss design, integration, and testing.

Exercises

1. List three key components of an AI development pipeline and describe their respective roles in the model lifecycle.

2. Describe the fundamental differences between functional and non-functional requirements in AI systems, providing examples of each category.

3. Explain how configuration control contributes to model reliability and reproducibility throughout the AI pipeline.

4. Compare batch processing and streaming architectures in terms of their pipeline requirements, advantages, and limitations.

5. Identify the non-functional requirements most essential for AI components in regulated industries, explaining their significance.

6. Explain the benefits of using architectural patterns such as pipe-and-filter in AI systems, providing a concrete implementation example.

7. Develop comprehensive functional and non-functional requirements for different data store technologies in an AI context.

8. Research and summarize the attributes of well-written requirement specifications, specifically for machine learning systems.

References

1. Kreuzberger, D., Kühl, N., & Hirschl, S. (2022). Machine Learning Operations (MLOps): Overview, Definition, and Architecture. *IEEE Access*, 10, 66631-66648.

2. Mäkinen, S., Skogström, H., Laaksonen, E., & Mikkonen, T. (2021). Who Needs MLOps: What Data Scientists Seek to Accomplish and How Can MLOps Help? *IEEE/ACM 1st Workshop on AI Engineering - Software Engineering for AI*, 109-112.

3. Kästner, C., & Kang, E. (2020). Teaching Software Engineering for AI-Enabled Systems. *ACM/IEEE 42nd International Conference on Software Engineering: Software Engineering Education and Training*, 45-48.

Unlock this book's exclusive benefits now

UNLOCK NOW

Scan this QR code or go to https://packtpub.com/unlock, then search this book by name.

Note: Keep your purchase invoice ready before you start.

6

Design, Integration, and Testing

How is it that we can declare Mozart's and Beethoven's composed music as masterpieces? Was this determined by people merely reading the sheet music? Of course not – we acknowledge these composers' brilliance when we actually hear the music. Similarly, while an architecture may be well conceived, it remains merely a paper artifact until executed.

This chapter provides practical insights into how architecture supports the design, integration, and testing phases of AI system development. We focus on the production pipeline because the development pipeline is often domain-dependent and not intended for production environments.

In this chapter, we will discuss the following:

- Design fundamentals
- System mode and state identification
- Logical component definition
- System tactics and patterns
- Integration approaches
- Testing

Design fundamentals

Design is the definition of components, their relationships, and processes in a specific configuration that aligns with an underlying architecture. Let's explore the most relevant design from major artifacts, including requirements, use cases, modes, patterns, and tactics.

Requirements

Building a production pipeline requires defining the requirements the pipeline must meet. Several requirement classes exist that collectively ensure the system satisfies both the functional and non-functional aspects needed for production-grade operation.

Performance requirements

Performance requirements focus on transactions, volumes, transformations, and processing execution time. These metrics establish clear thresholds for acceptable performance and aspirational targets for optimal operation:

Metric	Description	Threshold	Objective
AP-1	Total time to conduct data cleansing	30 secs/GB	10 secs/GB
AP-2	Total time to conduct data transformations	30 secs/GB	10 secs/GB
AP-3	Time to execute the model	10 secs	5 secs
AP-4	Time to write to the results store	5 secs/GB	3 secs/GB
AP-5	Time to write to end user stores	5 secs/GB	3 secs/GB
AP-6	Data store transactions	10,000 events/sec	20,000 events/sec
AP-7	Machine learning model accuracy	.88	.94
AP-8	Machine learning **Area Under Curve (AUC)**	.9	.95
AP-9	Time to update pipeline operations	1 sec	.5 secs
AP-10	Time to reconfigure to safe configuration	1 sec	.5 secs
AP-11	Model fairness across demographic groups	90% parity	95% parity
AP-12	Model explainability score	0.7	0.8
AP-13	Model robustness to input perturbations	±10% accuracy change	±5% accuracy change

Non-functional requirements

Non-functional requirements focus on the pipeline's continued operation capability. These requirements ensure the system remains resilient, responsive, and reliable throughout its operational life cycle:

Metric	Description	Threshold	Objective
NF-1	Availability – uptime	> 99.9%	> 99.99%
NF-2	Time to restore upon error	< 1 min	< 30 secs

NF-3	No single point of failure	N/A	N/A
NF-4	Time to update pipeline	< 3 mins	< 1 min
NF-5	Time to detect fault	< .5 secs	< .1 secs
NF-6	Deploy security patch	< 600 secs	< 180 secs
NF-7	Report pipeline health updates	< 10 secs	< 5 secs
NF-8	Model drift detection delay	< 1 hour	< 10 mins
NF-9	Feature pipeline isolation	N/A	N/A

Security requirements

Security considerations must include model security. Modern AI systems face unique security challenges beyond traditional software, including model extraction attacks and adversarial inputs:

Metric	Description	Threshold	Objective
SEC-1	The pipeline shall use a public key infrastructure for external interfaces	N/A	N/A
SEC-2	The pipeline shall record all users' date, time, and executions performed in the pipeline	N/A	N/A
SEC-3	All hardware shall be able to be updated for security patches without interference from pipeline operations	N/A	N/A
SEC-4	The pipeline shall protect models against adversarial attacks	N/A	N/A
SEC-5	The pipeline shall implement data access controls to prevent unauthorized data access	N/A	N/A
SEC-6	The pipeline shall monitor for model extraction attacks	N/A	N/A

Compliance requirements

Pipeline operations often automate processes and decisions, requiring specific compliance measures. As AI systems increasingly make or influence high-stakes decisions, regulatory compliance becomes a critical design consideration:

Metric	Description	Threshold	Objective
CP-1	The pipeline shall only allow authorized users to view customers' personal data	N/A	N/A
CP-2	All financial transactions shall be archived	N/A	N/A
CP-3	All financial identification information shall be encrypted at rest	N/A	N/A

CP-4	All financial identification information shall be encrypted when in use	N/A	N/A
CP-5	All model decisions shall maintain complete audit trails	N/A	N/A
CP-6	All model versions shall be logged in the model registry with lineage	N/A	N/A
CP-7	The pipeline shall support model governance review workflows	N/A	N/A

Actors and use cases

Production pipeline complexity becomes evident when examining high-level use cases. The AI pipeline system involves interactions between multiple stakeholders, each with specific roles and responsibilities in the overall ecosystem.

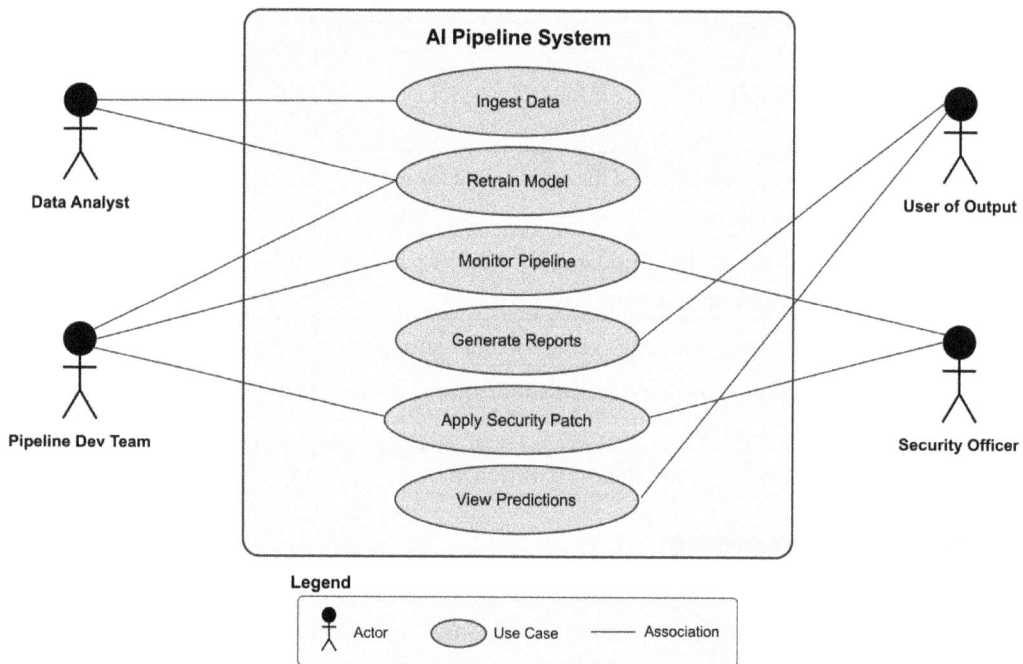

Figure 6.1: AI pipeline system: Use case diagram

Figure 6.1 illustrates the interactions between key actors and primary use cases within an AI pipeline system. The diagram shows four principal actors: data analysts who primarily work with data ingestion and model retraining; pipeline development teams who oversee monitoring, report generation, and security patches; security officers who focus on security patch management; and users of output who consume the model predictions. The interconnected use cases demonstrate how these actors collaborate across the system's functional boundaries.

This use case diagram serves as an anchor for understanding system scope and actor responsibilities. Each oval represents a distinct piece of functionality required by the system, while the connecting lines indicate which actors interact with each capability. For system architects, this visualization helps establish clear boundaries and identify potential areas where components might need to communicate or share resources.

The key actors identified in AI pipeline systems are the following:

1. **Data analyst**: Responsible for data preparation, feature engineering, and model validation
2. **Users of output**: Consumers of the model's predictions and insights
3. **Pipeline development team**: Engineers who build and maintain the pipeline infrastructure
4. **Operations team**: Professionals who ensure the day-to-day reliability of the system
5. **Consumers of pipeline development team**: Stakeholders who provide requirements to the development team
6. **Site reliability engineers**: Specialists in maintaining system stability and performance
7. **Model validators**: Experts who verify model accuracy and fairness
8. **Security officers**: Professionals responsible for protecting system assets and data
9. **Compliance officers**: Specialists who ensure adherence to regulatory requirements

A comprehensive use case template should include contextual information to guide implementation and testing. The template typically includes the use case identifier, a descriptive title using action verbs, detailed context, primary actor identification, pre- and post-conditions, main success scenario, potential extensions, frequency of use estimation, ownership assignment across teams, and relative priority to guide implementation sequencing.

System modes

The design process must capture different system modes that reflect various operational states an AI system might inhabit. Modern AI systems require sophisticated state management to handle transitions between different modes of operation.

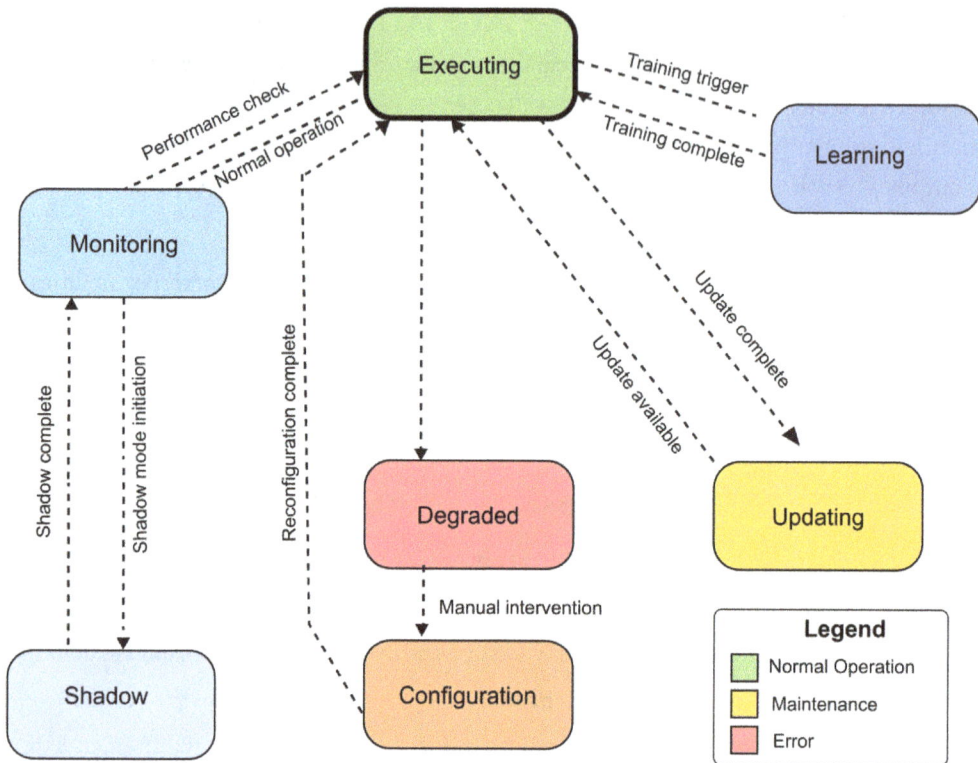

Figure 6.2: System modes state diagram

🔍**Quick tip**: Need to see a high-resolution version of this image? Open this book in the next-gen Packt Reader or view it in the PDF/ePub copy.

🔖**The next-gen Packt Reader** and a **free PDF/ePub copy** of this book are included with your purchase. Scan the QR code OR visit `https://packtpub.com/unlock`, then use the search bar to find this book by name. Double-check the edition shown to make sure you get the right one.

Figure 6.2 provides a comprehensive visualization of how an AI pipeline transitions between different operational states. The central **Executing** mode (shown in green) represents normal operation, with various transition paths connecting to specialized operational modes. The blue states (**Monitoring**, **Learning**, and **Shadow**) represent different operational variants where the system performs additional functions while maintaining service. The yellow **Updating** state indicates when the system is undergoing maintenance or modifications, while the red **Degraded** state represents error conditions where full functionality is compromised. The orange **Configuration** state typically follows manual intervention from the degraded state.

This state diagram serves multiple purposes in the design process. First, it helps engineers understand which transitions must be explicitly handled in the system implementation. Second, it establishes recovery paths from error states back to normal operation. Third, it provides operations teams with a mental model for troubleshooting when system behavior deviates from expectations.

Modern AI systems commonly implement the following operational modes:

- **Executing mode** serves as the primary operational state where the system processes incoming requests and generates predictions or insights using the deployed models. This represents the normal, steady-state operation of the system.

- **Monitoring mode** focuses on observing system behavior, model performance, and data quality without necessarily making changes. This mode enables continuous assessment of the pipeline's health and effectiveness.

- **Learning mode** activates when models are being updated with new data or when hyperparameter tuning is taking place. During this state, the system may allocate additional resources to training processes while maintaining inference capabilities.

- **Shadow mode** enables new models to run alongside production models without affecting user-facing outputs. This allows comparison of alternative models' performance under real-world conditions without risking production impact.

- **Degraded mode** represents a state where the system continues to function but with reduced capabilities or performance. This might occur during component failures or resource constraints, requiring graceful degradation strategies.

- **Updating mode** occurs when system components are being modified, replaced, or enhanced. Careful management of this state is essential to minimize service disruptions during upgrades.

- **Configuration mode** represents system setup or reconfiguration, often requiring specialized access and validation procedures to ensure changes don't compromise system integrity or security.

We will now shift to the development of logical modeling, where we look to visually capture the main system components and their associated relationships.

Block definition diagrams

Using a pipeline architecture as a starting point, we define key components of the development pipeline. Each component addresses specific functional requirements while contributing to the overall system capabilities.

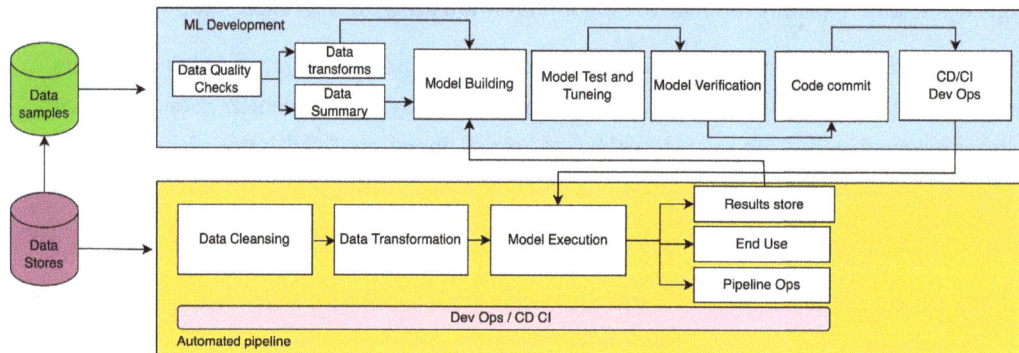

Figure 6.3: Block definition diagram for a pipeline system

Data cleansing

The data cleansing functionality ensures incoming pipeline data is of the highest quality. In production AI systems, data quality directly impacts model performance and system reliability. Modern implementations include automated data validation pipelines that can detect schema violations and format inconsistencies; anomaly detection frameworks capable of identifying outliers and potentially erroneous values; and data quality enforcement mechanisms that apply predefined rules to standardize, normalize, or correct problematic data points.

Data cleansing components often incorporate feedback loops that improve over time, learning from patterns of data issues to anticipate and address common problems. These systems must balance thoroughness with performance considerations, as excessive cleansing operations can create bottlenecks in high-throughput environments.

Data transformation

The data transformation functionality processes incoming data streams to prepare them for the AI model. This critical pipeline stage converts cleansed data into formats optimized for model consumption. Contemporary AI systems might implement feature stores that centralize feature computation and enable feature reuse across multiple models, automated feature engineering capabilities that can discover and generate relevant features from raw data, and vector embedding generation services that convert structured or unstructured data into dimensional vector spaces suitable for deep learning models.

Effective data transformation components maintain transformation consistency between training and inference pipelines, ensuring that models encounter the same feature distributions in both contexts. They also typically provide versioning capabilities to track how transformation logic evolves over time, enabling reproducibility and facilitating debugging.

Machine learning model

The machine learning functionality processes input data to generate inferences, regressions, or other data summaries. As the analytical core of the AI pipeline, this component encompasses not just the model itself but the surrounding infrastructure to support its deployment and operation. Production-grade implementations include model registry integration for versioning and lineage tracking, sophisticated A/B testing frameworks that enable controlled experimentation with model variants, and explainability components that provide insights into model decisions.

Model components in mature AI systems provide consistent interfaces that abstract away implementation details, allowing different algorithms or approaches to be swapped without disrupting downstream consumers. They also incorporate monitoring hooks that expose performance metrics and internal state information for operational visibility.

Pipeline operations

The pipeline operations functionality collects status from other pipeline parts and visualizes pipeline operations. This component serves as the nervous system of the AI pipeline, providing observability and control capabilities. Modern MLOps platforms extend basic monitoring with automated alerting systems that detect anomalies or performance degradation, self-healing capabilities that can address common issues without manual intervention, and sophisticated visualizations that help operators understand complex system behaviors.

Pipeline operations components must balance comprehensive monitoring with performance impact considerations, as excessive instrumentation can create overhead. They typically implement configurable logging levels and sampling strategies to manage this trade-off while still providing actionable insights when needed.

Results store

The results store provides a central point for model results and indexing. This component serves as both the output destination for model predictions and a historical repository enabling analysis and audit capabilities. Modern implementations include feature attribution storage that captures which input features most influenced specific predictions, decision explanation logging that documents reasoning chains or confidence levels, and integration with business intelligence platforms that enable stakeholders to derive insights from aggregated prediction data.

Effective results store implementations must balance performance considerations with retention policies, often implementing tiered storage strategies that maintain recent results in high-performance stores while archiving older data in more cost-effective solutions. They also typically implement access controls that restrict sensitive prediction data to authorized users while enabling appropriate analytical access.

System tactics and patterns

Software tactics and patterns drive overall software architecture toward a cohesive design. A tactic is a general principle, while a pattern is a specific realization of that principle. Together, they provide design guidance that helps architects achieve desired quality attributes. The concepts described here are elaborated on and come from the excellent reference book by Bass et al. [1].

Key attributes

Two particularly important high-level attributes are maintainability and availability, which address the system's evolution over time and its resilience to failures, respectively.

Maintainability tactics and patterns

Maintainability encompasses the system's capacity to accommodate changes, undergo testing, adapt to new requirements, and support configuration management. This quality attribute breaks down into several tactical areas:

1. **Modifiability** focuses on minimizing the cost of change through tactics such as component isolation, abstraction, and standardized interfaces. In AI systems, this might manifest as clearly separated data processing, model training, and inference pipelines that can evolve independently.

2. **Testability** enables effective verification through introspection points, test harnesses, and sandboxed environments. AI systems benefit from specialized testability features such as model versioning, prediction explanations, and dataset versioning that support reproducible evaluations.

3. **Adaptability** allows the system to accommodate changing environments or requirements without significant rework. Techniques include plugin architectures, feature toggles, and configuration-driven behavior. In AI contexts, this might include model architecture abstraction layers that allow algorithm swapping without pipeline modifications.

4. **Configurability** provides mechanisms to alter system behavior without code changes. This typically involves externalized configuration, parameter management systems, and dynamic reconfiguration capabilities. AI systems often extend these with model hyperparameter management and feature flag systems.

Availability tactics and patterns

Availability addresses the system's ability to deliver service when needed, focusing on preventing, detecting, and recovering from failures. This quality attribute centers on fault-centric tactics:

1. **Fault detection** involves monitoring, heartbeats, and exception handling to identify when components deviate from expected behavior. AI systems often implement specialized detection for concept drift, data quality issues, and model performance degradation.

2. **Fault recovery** encompasses tactics such as redundancy, rollback, and graceful degradation that help systems return to operational status after failures. In AI pipelines, this might include model fallback mechanisms, prediction caching, human in the loop, and automated retraining workflows.

3. **Fault prevention** focuses on avoiding failures through input validation, resource isolation, and transaction integrity controls. AI-specific prevention tactics include adversarial example detection, robust feature processing, and model verification before deployment.

Essential patterns for AI systems

Several architectural patterns prove particularly valuable in AI system design, each addressing specific quality attribute challenges.

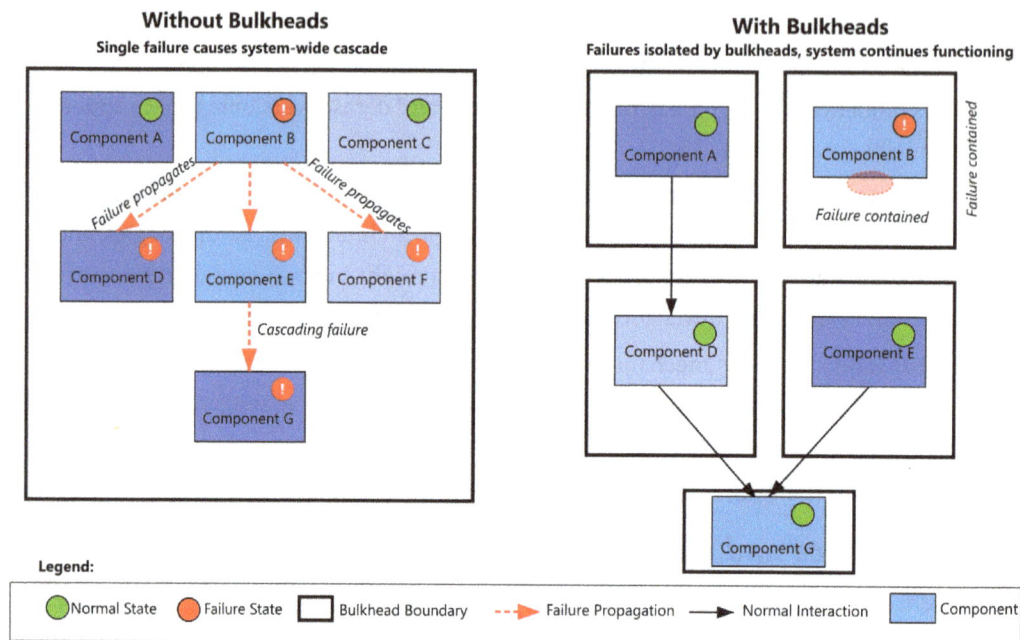

Without Bulkheads
Single failure causes system-wide cascade

With Bulkheads
Failures isolated by bulkheads, system continues functioning

Figure 6.4: Bulkhead pattern visualization

Figure 6.4 illustrates one of the most critical resilience patterns for AI systems. On the left side, we see a system without bulkheads where a single component failure (**Component B**) triggers a cascading failure throughout the system as the error propagates unchecked. On the right, the same component failure occurs but remains contained within its isolation boundary, allowing the rest of the system to continue functioning normally.

The bulkhead pattern, borrowed from naval architecture where ships are divided into compartments to prevent a single breach from sinking the entire vessel, involves partitioning system components to prevent failures from cascading. This visualization demonstrates how isolation boundaries around components limit the "blast radius" of failures, enabling graceful degradation rather than complete system failure. Modern implementations might include containerization, service boundaries with circuit breakers, or process isolation techniques.

For AI systems handling critical workloads, bulkheads become essential when implementing high-availability architectures. They're particularly valuable in model-serving infrastructure, where a problematic model should not affect other models or shared resources.

Beyond bulkheads, several other patterns prove valuable in AI systems:

- The **Service-Oriented pattern** enables extensibility by organizing functionality into distinct services with well-defined interfaces. This allows new capabilities to be added without disrupting existing components. In AI systems, this might manifest as separate feature services, model services, and explanation services that can evolve independently.

- The **Balancer pattern** distributes load across multiple resources to prevent overloading and ensure consistent performance. AI systems often implement specialized balancing for compute-intensive operations such as training and inference, with awareness of hardware acceleration requirements.

- The **Fail and Repeat pattern** implements retry logic with appropriate backoff strategies to handle transient failures. This is particularly valuable in distributed AI systems where network partitions or resource contention might cause temporary unavailability.

- The **Throttle pattern** controls resource utilization by limiting processing rates or concurrent operations. In AI contexts, this helps manage expensive operations such as inference on specialized hardware or database accesses for feature retrieval.

- The **Circuit pattern** (also known as the circuit breaker) monitors for failure conditions and temporarily disables operations when failures exceed thresholds. This prevents system overload during recovery and allows graceful degradation during partial outages.

- The **N-Party Voting Control pattern** distributes decision authority across multiple components, requiring consensus for critical operations. In AI systems, this might manifest as ensemble models where multiple algorithms must agree on predictions, or federated validation of data quality.

Modern AI systems have also developed specialized patterns addressing unique challenges:

- The **Feature Store pattern** centralizes feature computation and storage, enabling consistent feature definitions across training and serving while reducing redundant computation. This pattern supports feature reuse across multiple models and provides a central point for monitoring feature drift.

- The **Champion-Challenger pattern** (also known as A/B testing) allows controlled evaluation of new models against current production models. This pattern enables data-driven decisions about model updates while managing risk.

- The **Shadow Deployment pattern** runs new models in parallel with production models, capturing predictions for comparison without actually using them for decisions. This provides real-world performance data without operational risk.

- The **Drift Detection pattern** continuously monitors distributions of inputs and outputs to identify when models are becoming less effective due to changing conditions. This pattern enables proactive model updates before performance significantly degrades.

- The **Explainability Wrapper pattern** augments model outputs with interpretable information about prediction rationale. This addresses transparency requirements while allowing the use of complex models.

- The **Canary Deployment pattern** gradually routes increasing portions of traffic to new model versions, enabling progressive validation with limited exposure to potential issues.

We will now shift our discussion to integration and testing, where the many interacting components of the system are brought together to realize a unified system.

Integration and testing

While architects don't play a major role in integration – primarily done by implementation engineers – integration issues inevitably arise. Architects are consulted to aid in design changes while maintaining system conceptual integrity.

Types of integrations

Several integration approaches exist, each with distinct advantages and challenges for AI system development.

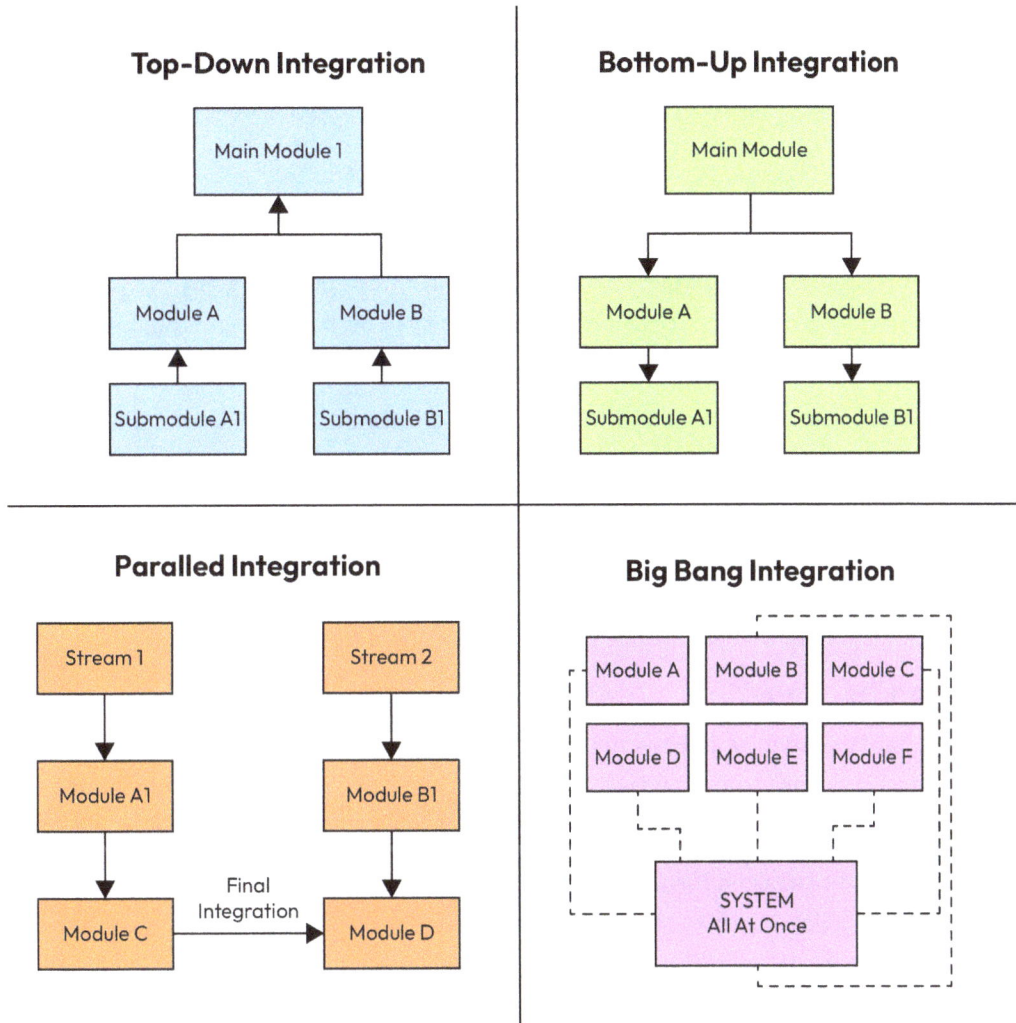

Figure 6.5: Integration approaches comparison

Figure 6.5 provides a visual comparison of four common integration strategies. The top-down approach (blue) begins with the main module and progressively integrates lower-level components, allowing early validation of high-level architectural concepts. The bottom-up approach (green) starts with the smallest components and builds upward, ensuring well-tested foundations before system-level integration begins.

The parallel approach (orange) develops independent integration streams that eventually merge at a final integration point, enabling team distribution and concurrent development. Finally, the "big bang" approach (purple) attempts to integrate all components simultaneously, which simplifies planning but introduces significant debugging challenges when issues arise.

Each approach has distinct trade-offs. Top-down integration provides earlier visibility into architectural issues but requires complex stubs or mocks for incomplete components. Bottom-up integration builds on solid, tested components but delays system-level testing. Parallel integration enables team distribution but introduces coordination challenges. Big bang integration simplifies planning but complicates debugging when multiple integration issues occur simultaneously.

Modern AI systems often implement hybrid approaches combining elements from multiple strategies. For instance, a team might use bottom-up integration for individual pipeline components while applying a parallel approach for separate data-processing and model-serving pipelines. Continuous integration practices have largely supplanted these discrete approaches in many development environments, with automated build and test pipelines continuously integrating components as they evolve.

Integration harness

An integration harness serves as a digital twin of the production pipeline, providing controlled environments for component testing and integration verification. Effective harnesses implement several key capabilities to support AI system integration.

First, they provide mechanisms for mimicking data inputs and instrumenting component interactions, allowing developers to simulate various scenarios without affecting production systems. They isolate module performance through controlled environments, enabling precise measurement of resource utilization and timing characteristics critical for AI components.

Integration harnesses also measure data storage and read/write patterns, identifying potential bottlenecks or inefficiencies before they impact production systems. They support data integrity testing without requiring full pipeline integration, allowing data-focused validation to proceed independently of component development.

For teams working in parallel, integration harnesses define stub interfaces that enable development against incomplete dependencies. They also provide specific logging points throughout the pipeline, facilitating debugging and performance analysis during integration activities.

Modern AI systems extend these traditional harness concepts with specialized capabilities, including containerized environments that ensure consistency across development and production, mock model servers that mimic inference behavior without requiring full models, synthetic data generators that produce realistic test data with known characteristics, feature stores and model registries that maintain versioned artifacts, and shadow deployment capabilities that enable side-by-side comparison of alternative implementations.

Testing types

The amount and type of testing needed depend on the machine learning system's criticality, complexity, and compliance requirements. AI systems require specialized testing approaches beyond traditional software validation.

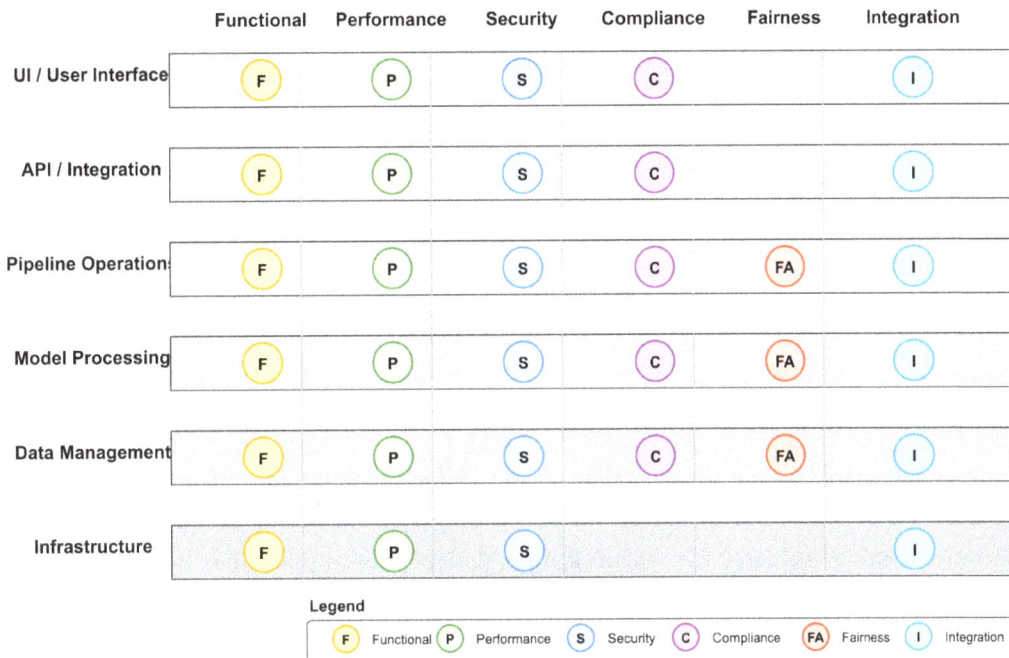

Figure 6.6: Testing scope diagram

Figure 6.6 presents a comprehensive testing coverage matrix for AI pipeline components. The matrix maps system layers (from **UI/User Interface** through **Infrastructure**) against testing types (**Functional, Performance, Security, Compliance, Fairness,** and **Integration**). Each cell indicates whether a particular testing type applies to that system layer.

This visualization highlights several important patterns in AI system testing. First, it shows that all system layers require multiple testing types – no single test approach is sufficient for any component. Second, it reveals that some testing concerns (such as **Fairness**) apply primarily to pipeline operations, model processing, and data management, but not to UI/API layers or infrastructure. Third, it emphasizes that integration testing spans all system layers, reflecting the interconnected nature of AI systems.

The testing scope diagram serves as a planning tool for test strategies, helping teams ensure comprehensive coverage across both system layers and quality attributes. It's particularly valuable for identifying gaps in test coverage or areas where specialized testing approaches might be needed.

Requirements testing

Requirements testing verifies that a system realizes its expected major functionality. For AI systems, this encompasses several specialized areas beyond traditional software validation.

Model accuracy and performance metrics verification ensure the system meets specified thresholds for predictive power using appropriate evaluation metrics such as precision, recall, F1 score, or mean squared error. Fairness testing across different groups validates that the model performs consistently for different demographic segments, avoiding disparate impact or algorithmic bias.

Robustness testing examines the system's resilience to input variations, including adversarial examples or perturbations that might confuse the model. Explainability capabilities testing verifies that the system can provide appropriate levels of transparency about its decision-making process, particularly for high-stakes decisions.

Data privacy safeguards testing confirms that sensitive information is appropriately protected throughout the pipeline, with proper access controls and anonymization where required. Ethical consideration testing evaluates the system against defined ethical guidelines or principles, ensuring alignment with organizational values and societal expectations.

Use case and scenario testing

Use case and scenario testing exercises the system as it will actually perform during operation, validating end-to-end functionality rather than isolated components. For AI systems, this includes specialized scenarios reflecting their unique operational characteristics.

Model performance testing across different input distributions examines how the system handles various data profiles, including edge cases and unusual patterns. Automated retraining workflow validation ensures that model update processes function correctly, maintaining model quality over time without manual intervention.

Feature pipeline execution testing verifies that data transformation processes correctly prepare inputs for model consumption with appropriate handling of missing values, outliers, and categorical encodings. Model monitoring behavior validation examines how the system detects and responds to drift, performance degradation, or other operational concerns.

Graceful degradation testing under load ensures the system maintains acceptable performance even as request volumes approach or exceed capacity limits, potentially leveraging fallback models or cached predictions when necessary.

Load testing

Load testing exercises the full technology span under realistic or stress conditions, identifying bottlenecks and performance limitations before they impact production systems. For AI pipelines, several specialized load testing scenarios are particularly relevant.

Inference latency testing under concurrent requests measures how model-serving performance changes as multiple users or systems simultaneously request predictions. Training throughput testing with large datasets evaluates how efficiently the system can process training data, identifying potential optimizations for computational efficiency.

Feature computation at scale testing examines how data transformation processes handle high volumes or velocities of incoming data. Online learning scenario testing validates how the system performs when simultaneously processing incoming data and updating models. Batch processing performance testing measures efficiency when processing large volumes of data in non-interactive contexts.

Model prediction testing

Model prediction testing verifies that model outputs match those from the model creation process, ensuring consistency between development and production environments. This testing category includes several specialized approaches for AI systems.

Adversarial testing examines model behavior when presented with intentionally problematic inputs designed to cause incorrect predictions. Concept drift simulation tests how models respond to gradually changing data distributions similar to those they might encounter in production over time.

Counterfactual testing evaluates model predictions against "what if" scenarios where input features are systematically varied to understand decision boundaries and model sensitivity. Slice-based testing across data subpopulations examines model performance for specific segments of the data, identifying potential weaknesses for particular use cases or user groups.

Ensemble consistency checking verifies that multiple models combined in ensemble architectures produce appropriately harmonized outputs without contradictions or inconsistencies.

Data quality testing

Data quality testing ensures pipeline resilience to errors and corruption in input data. This testing category is particularly important for AI systems, where data quality directly impacts model performance and system reliability.

Automated schema validation testing verifies that incoming data adheres to expected formats and type constraints. Data drift detection testing validates that monitoring systems correctly identify when input distributions change significantly from training data. Missing value handling testing examines how the pipeline processes incomplete data, ensuring graceful handling without system failures.

Outlier processing testing verifies appropriate treatment of extreme values that might otherwise disproportionately influence model behavior. Data lineage tracking testing confirms that the system maintains appropriate metadata about data origins and transformations, supporting auditability and debugging.

Error and fault recovery testing

Error and fault recovery testing ensures system resilience in the face of component failures or unexpected conditions. For AI systems with high-availability requirements, several specialized testing approaches are relevant.

Model fallback mechanism testing verifies that the system can switch to alternative models when primary models fail or perform poorly. Feature pipeline isolation testing confirms that failures in feature computation for one model don't affect other models sharing the pipeline. Model registry failover testing validates that the system can retrieve models from alternative sources if the primary registry becomes unavailable.

Circuit breaker behavior verification examines how the system detects and responds to persistent failure conditions, including appropriate service disabling and recovery procedures. Graceful degradation testing under component failure ensures the system maintains core functionality even when some components are unavailable or performing suboptimally.

Compliance testing

Compliance testing ensures legal regulations and requirements aren't overlooked in system implementation. For AI systems making or influencing decisions with regulatory implications, this testing category becomes particularly important.

Model governance workflow verification confirms that approval and documentation processes meet organizational and regulatory requirements. Bias testing across protected groups examines model behavior for potential discrimination based on sensitive attributes such as race, gender, or age.

Explainability testing for high-risk decisions validates that the system can provide sufficient transparency for decisions with significant consequences. Audit trail completeness testing confirms that the system captures all required information for accountability and regulatory review.

Data privacy and protection measures testing verifies appropriate handling of sensitive information throughout the pipeline. Regulatory documentation generation testing confirms that the system can produce required reports and disclosures for compliance purposes.

User interface testing

User interface testing focuses on the effectiveness of the interfaces used by operators and stakeholders to understand system behavior and results. For AI systems, several specialized interface types require validation.

Model monitoring dashboard testing evaluates whether operators can effectively understand model health and performance through visual interfaces. Explainability visualization tool testing confirms that stakeholders can interpret model decisions through appropriate visual representations of feature importance or decision logic.

Alert triage interface testing examines how effectively operators can identify, prioritize, and respond to system alerts or anomalies. Model comparison tool testing validates interfaces that allow side-by-side evaluation of different models or model versions.

Data quality monitoring display testing confirms that data issues are effectively communicated to the appropriate stakeholders. Debugging tool testing for model behavior validates that developers and data scientists can effectively troubleshoot unexpected model outputs or performance issues.

Continuous development and integration

Continuous integration is critical for developing robust machine learning pipeline operations. Modern AI systems extend traditional CI/CD practices with specialized capabilities addressing their unique development characteristics.

Automated model validation pipelines ensure that models meet quality thresholds before deployment, including accuracy, fairness, and robustness checks. Feature validation tests verify that data transformations produce expected distributions and formats, maintaining consistency between training and serving.

Data quality gates prevent contamination of production systems with problematic data by automatically validating incoming data against defined quality criteria. Model performance regression testing compares new models against existing baselines to ensure improvements in some areas don't come at the cost of degradation in others.

A/B testing frameworks enable controlled experiments with model variants, collecting performance data to inform deployment decisions. Canary deployment automation gradually increases traffic to new models while monitoring for issues, enabling risk-managed rollouts. Rollback mechanisms provide emergency restoration of previous versions when unexpected issues arise after deployment.

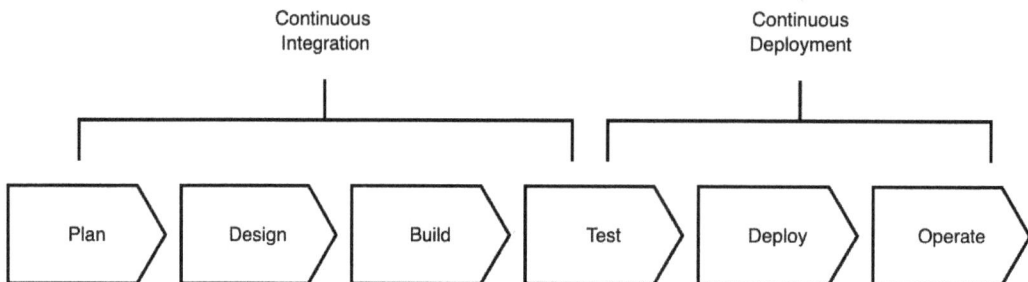

Figure 6.7: Continuous integration and continuous deployment pipeline

Summary

This chapter has explored the critical journey from architectural concepts to functioning AI systems through design, integration, and testing. Much like a musical composition that remains theoretical until performed, AI architectures must be realized through thoughtful design decisions, systematic integration approaches, and comprehensive testing strategies to deliver their intended value.

The *Design fundamentals* section established how requirements, use cases, and system modes form the foundation for translating architectural vision into concrete components. The use case diagram (*Figure 6.1*) illustrated the complex interactions between diverse stakeholders and system functionality, while the system modes state diagram (*Figure 6.2*) mapped the operational states an AI system must navigate throughout its life cycle.

Block definition diagrams detailed the core components of AI pipelines – data cleansing, data transformation, machine learning models, pipeline operations, and results storage – each addressing specific functional requirements while contributing to the system's overall capabilities. These components must be designed with both their individual responsibilities and their collaborative interactions in mind.

System tactics and patterns provide proven approaches for achieving quality attributes such as maintainability and availability. The bulkhead pattern visualization (*Figure 6.4*) demonstrated how architectural decisions directly impact system resilience, showing how isolation boundaries prevent cascading failures that might otherwise compromise entire systems.

The integration approaches comparison (*Figure 6.5*) revealed the trade-offs between top-down, bottom-up, parallel, and big bang strategies, highlighting how modern AI systems often adopt hybrid approaches tailored to their specific development contexts. Integration harnesses provide controlled environments for verifying component interactions before production deployment.

The testing scope diagram (*Figure 6.6*) presented a comprehensive matrix of testing types across system layers, emphasizing that AI systems require multi-faceted validation strategies addressing functional correctness, performance, security, compliance, fairness, and integration concerns. Specialized testing approaches for requirements, use cases, load conditions, model predictions, data quality, error handling, compliance, and user interfaces collectively ensure system quality.

Throughout this evolution from architecture to implementation, the role of the architect remains critical – not as the primary implementer, but as the guardian of conceptual integrity who ensures that design decisions and implementation trade-offs align with the system's architectural vision and quality attributes. As AI systems grow increasingly complex and consequential, this architectural guidance becomes ever more essential to create systems that not only function as specified but deliver lasting value in production environments.

In the next chapter, we will delve into a case study that looks to bring many of the concepts discussed throughout the book into focus.

Exercises

1. Create class diagrams for the data ingest block diagram.
2. Develop data flow diagrams for inputs and outputs to the model execution component.
3. Develop block diagrams for the maintainability non-functional requirement.
4. Develop block diagrams for the availability non-functional requirement.
5. Pick three use cases and actors and fully develop the use cases.

6. Define a set of tests that would show fault and error handling for data ingestion and model execution.

7. Describe how to simulate high data loads for pipeline load testing.

8. Pick two use cases from Chapter 5 and determine how tests would be defined.

9. Define two tests for ensuring that the data quality part of a pipeline is working correctly.

10. For your domain, define a test that ensures a compliance requirement will be met.

11. Design a test to verify that a machine learning model meets fairness requirements across different demographic groups.

12. Develop a test plan for validating model explainability capabilities in a high-stakes decision-making context.

13. Design a monitoring system for detecting and alerting on model drift in production.

References

1. Bass, L., Clements, P., & Kazman, R. (2021). *Software Architecture in Practice* (4th ed.). Addison-Wesley Professional.

7

Architecting a Generative AI System — A Case Study

Throughout this book, we have explored core principles of AI system architecture, focusing on managing complexity, ensuring scalability, and integrating AI technologies into enterprise software. We examined how software engineering best practices, such as modular design and structured data pipelines, help optimize AI-enabled systems. We also addressed challenges such as aligning AI applications with stakeholder expectations, implementing effective design patterns, and adopting iterative development cycles that adjust to changing data and business needs. Case studies and real-world examples provided a structured framework for balancing technical precision with flexibility.

This final chapter focuses on generative AI and **Large Language Models (LLMs)** as a case study in applying architectural best practices to real-world AI deployments. We will walk through the design of an LLM-powered customer support knowledge management system, incorporating **Retrieval-Augmented Generation (RAG)**, search capabilities, and adaptive learning. By analyzing key components such as AI agents, vector databases, and web search integrations, we will connect these technologies to foundational architectural strategies, including modularity, data pipeline efficiency, and cloud scalability. This example provides a clear path from high-level business goals to a validated AI system.

In this chapter, we will cover the following topics:

- Framing a problem of a company designing its knowledge platform and investigating the potential to use generative AI
- How to translate the company's requirements into data science objectives
- Explaining the possible architecture choices
- Designing an LLM-centric solution for the company's knowledge platform
- How to quantify the quality of generative AI-centric design

By the end of this chapter, you will have a structured, practical understanding of how generative AI can be effectively designed and deployed in enterprise settings, with a focus on scalability, compliance, and long-term sustainability.

The business challenge: Knowledge management crisis

TechSolve, our case study ERP provider, serving diverse enterprise clients across manufacturing, retail, and healthcare sectors, faces a significant knowledge management challenge that threatens both operational efficiency and client relationships:

- **Fragmented knowledge ecosystem**: Critical information scattered across 12+ siloed systems, including legacy documentation, modern wikis, support tickets, and communication platforms.
- **Inefficient resource utilization**: Support engineers waste 60% of their time searching for information rather than applying expertise to solve client problems.
- **Institutional knowledge erosion**: Key insights and troubleshooting wisdom walk out the door as experienced staff depart, with an estimated 15% of critical knowledge undocumented.
- **Extended response times**: Customer resolution times have stretched to an average of three days, significantly exceeding SLAs and endangering seven-figure enterprise client relationships.
- **Diminishing service quality**: A self-reinforcing cycle where exhausted engineers deliver declining service quality, further increasing ticket volumes and customer dissatisfaction

The financial implications are substantial: TechSolve estimates these inefficiencies cost $3.2 million annually through additional staffing requirements, lost productivity, and customer churn. More concerning is the competitive disadvantage as nimbler competitors leverage AI to provide superior support experiences.

The vision: Transformation through generative AI

To address these challenges, TechSolve's executive team designs a comprehensive generative AI implementation leveraging LLMs to transform knowledge management across the organization:

- **Unified knowledge framework**: Consolidate information from multiple repositories into a single semantic index that spans formats, locations, and departments.

- **How indexing works**: Connectors pull unstructured content from **wikis, shared drives, email archives, ticket transcripts, PDFs**, and **chat logs**. Each item goes through normalization, OCR for scanned files, de-duplication, and canonical URL assignment. Content is **chunked into passage-sized spans**, embedded, and stored in the vector database with rich metadata such as **source, author, product, version, creation date, sensitivity flags**, and **PII tags**. Refreshing is a nightly job, and change data capture is carried out where available.

- **Grounded AI responses**: Implement RAG to anchor answers in verified sources while preserving the synthesizing power of LLMs.

- **Contextual intelligence**: Provide a conversational interface that understands domain terminology, technical relationships, and implicit knowledge needs.

- **Adaptive learning system**: Create a self-improving platform that refines prompts, retrieval strategies, and tool selection using user feedback and usage patterns.

- **Structured knowledge connectors**: Integrate **transactional systems** to fetch trusted facts. Read-only adapters connect to a **CRM** (for example, **Salesforce**), **ERP** (for example, **SAP**), and **ITSM** (for example, **ServiceNow**) to retrieve entitlements, product configurations, account status, case history, and SLAs. Access is enforced with **row-level security**, API rate limits, and caching or scheduled sync. Data is exposed to the agent as **typed tool calls** or **parameterized SQL views** so answers can cite both documents and system facts.

The initial prototype utilizes a LangChain agent that orchestrates retrieval and generation across tools [4], with semantic search and web integration providing current external context [3][7]. This architecture enables multi-step reasoning that can navigate complex support scenarios with minimal human intervention. The prototype included two pipelines: an **unstructured indexer** for wikis, emails, PDFs, and tickets, and **structured adapters** for CRM and ERP, which let the agent blend referenced documents with live system facts in a single cited response.

"This isn't simply about implementing an AI chatbot. We're fundamentally reimagining how institutional knowledge flows through our organization, breaking down silos that have accumulated over decades of growth," says Sarah Chen, the CTO at TechSolve.

Aligning business and technical objectives

The successful implementation of TechSolve's generative AI system required careful alignment between high-level business goals and specific technical capabilities. This alignment process ensured that all stakeholders – from executive leadership to engineering teams – shared a unified vision of success with clear performance indicators. By translating business imperatives into concrete data science and engineering objectives, TechSolve created a framework that guided decision-making throughout the project life cycle, from initial architecture design through deployment and continuous improvement.

Data science objectives

These business goals translate into five data science objectives with auditability, explainability, and confidence reporting aligned with AI risk management guidance [2][5]. Establishing these quantifiable metrics enabled TechSolve's data science team to evaluate model performance systematically and align technical implementation decisions with the overall business strategy. The following objectives translate TechSolve's business needs into measurable technical targets, providing clear direction for the data science team:

- **High-relevance retrieval**: Achieve 85% precision in identifying the most relevant knowledge fragments for a given query, with specialized metrics for technical versus procedural content.

- **Contextual understanding**: Attain 90% accuracy in identifying user intent, including implicit knowledge needs, technical context, and query reformulation requirements.

- **Response generation quality**: Limit inaccuracies to under 5% in generated responses, with strict factuality requirements for technical specifications and compatibility guidance.

- **Explainability**: Ensure all system responses include clear source citations and confidence levels, maintaining an audit trail from query to final response.

- **Continuous improvement**: Implement learning mechanisms that demonstrably improve system performance by 1–2% monthly based on usage patterns and explicit feedback.

These objectives establish the foundation for model selection, training methodologies, evaluation frameworks, and system architecture, while providing clear indicators of progress toward broader business outcomes.

The architecture: Core components and workflow

Developing an enterprise-scale generative AI system required TechSolve to integrate multiple specialized components into a cohesive architecture. This section examines the technical foundation that enabled the transformation of scattered knowledge repositories into a unified, responsive system capable of addressing complex support queries with accuracy and consistency.

System overview

TechSolve's generative AI architecture centers on LangChain, an orchestration framework that coordinates multiple AI components beyond simple LLM interactions. The system implements an intelligent agent that strategically manages user queries, determining which tools to employ and sequencing their execution for optimal results.

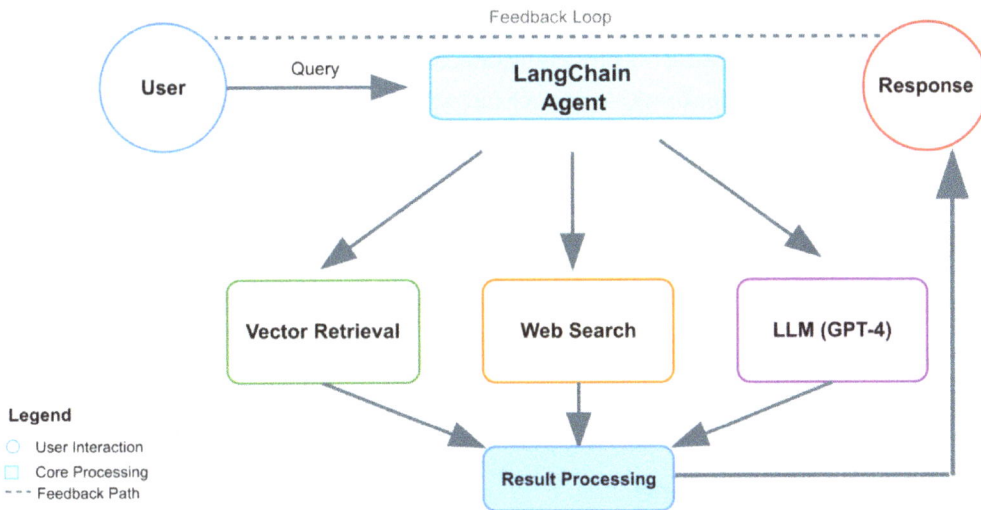

Figure 7.1: AI query processing workflow: Integrating LLMs with vector search and web data

🔍 **Quick tip:** Need to see a high-resolution version of this image? Open this book in the next-gen Packt Reader or view it in the PDF/ePub copy.

📖 **The next-gen Packt Reader** and a **free PDF/ePub copy** of this book are included with your purchase. Scan the QR code OR visit `https://packtpub.com/unlock`, then use the search bar to find this book by name. Double-check the edition shown to make sure you get the right one.

The workflow shown in *Figure 7.1* illustrates how user queries flow through the system, with the LangChain agent orchestrating the process by directing queries to appropriate tools: vector retrieval for accessing knowledge bases, web search for gathering external information, or directly to the LLM for processing. After response generation, a feedback loop enables continuous system improvement based on user interactions.

Key components

Now, we'll dive into the specific architectural components that make this system work. Each piece plays a crucial role in transforming user questions into accurate, helpful responses. Let's start with the brain of the operation and work our way through the supporting technologies that handle search and data retrieval.

LLM: The cognitive engine

Now, we'll dive into the specific architectural components that make this system work. Each piece plays a crucial role in transforming user questions into accurate, helpful responses. Let's start with the brain of the operation and work our way through the supporting technologies that handle search and data retrieval.

The LLM functions as the central cognitive engine, interpreting queries, formulating retrieval plans, integrating knowledge base data, and constructing coherent responses. TechSolve implemented a tiered approach:

- **Primary model**: OpenAI's GPT-4.1 for complex reasoning tasks requiring sophisticated understanding of technical concepts, troubleshooting workflows, and nuanced customer needs.

- **Secondary model**: GPT-4o mini takes care of routine inquiries, delivering significantly better cost efficiency than GPT-3.5-Turbo while maintaining high-quality responses for straightforward information retrieval.

- **Fallback model**: An internal deployment of Llama 2 70B for scenarios requiring operation during API outages or for handling sensitive data with specific security requirements. However, deploying a 70B parameter model locally comes with substantial infrastructure requirements. Organizations need to consider GPU memory demands, potential model quantization to 4-bit or 8-bit precision to reduce resource usage, and parameter pruning techniques that balance capability with hardware constraints. Many companies find that smaller models such as 7B or 13B variants provide adequate fallback performance while dramatically cutting hardware costs and complexity.

This multi-model architecture preserves maximum flexibility, preventing vendor lock-in while enabling adoption of emerging language models as the technology landscape evolves. Critical to this design is the abstraction layer, which standardizes inputs and outputs across models, allowing seamless switching based on query complexity, cost considerations, or specific compliance requirements.

Retrieval system (vector database): The knowledge repository

The vector database is the backbone of TechSolve's knowledge architecture, enabling semantic search across millions of document fragments. The vector database grounds responses through RAG, which combines external knowledge with generation [3]. TechSolve has selected Pinecone as the primary vector store because of its scalability, managed service model, and strong support for production workloads.

However, alternative options such as Qdrant could also be valuable, particularly in scenarios where cost optimization or fine-grained control over model tuning is a priority. Qdrant offers an open source path with strong customization features, which may appeal to organizations that prefer more flexibility in managing their own infrastructure.

Regardless of the specific platform, the core design principle remains the same: embeddings are generated, indexed, and retrieved efficiently to ground the LLM in accurate organizational knowledge.

- **Embedding framework**: Utilizes OpenAI's text-embedding-ada-002 model to convert the meaning of document fragments into 1,536-dimensional vectors. This process captures the "semantic essence" of the text, effectively giving each concept a numerical coordinate on a vast map of ideas. Documents with similar meanings will have coordinates that are close together, allowing the system to find related information even if the wording is different.

- **Vector storage**: Implements Pinecone as the primary vector database, with 16 million document chunks indexed across six separate indexes optimized for different content types

- **Hybrid retrieval**: Combines vector similarity search with BM25 keyword matching to balance semantic understanding with term specificity

- **Metadata filtering**: Enhances retrieval precision through filtering on 14 distinct metadata fields, including document age, author expertise level, content type, and relevance scores

This system forms the foundation for RAG, which has proven critical for reducing hallucinations by 87% in TechSolve's implementation by grounding AI outputs in verified, authoritative knowledge sources with clear provenance tracking.

In addition to RAG, some organizations also explore **Context-Aware Generation** (**CAG**). While RAG focuses on grounding answers with external sources, CAG optimizes how context is used within the model itself. This approach can reduce redundant retrieval calls, lower query costs, and improve response efficiency, making it a valuable addition in scenarios where performance and cost control are high priorities.

Web search integration: Real-time information access

To address knowledge cutoff limitations inherent in all pre-trained language models, the architecture incorporates web search integration:

- **API integration**: Leverages Google Programmable Search Engine through a custom wrapper that manages rate limiting, caching, and result filtering

- **Source credibility**: Implements a custom ranking algorithm that prioritizes authoritative sources such as official documentation, verified forums, and primary research

- **Content extraction**: Utilizes specialized scraping techniques to extract clean, relevant content from search results while preserving attribution

- **Result synthesis**: Applies text summarization techniques to distill key insights before incorporation into the final response

This component provides access to real-time information, ensuring up-to-date responses for rapidly evolving topics such as software updates, emerging issues, and community-developed solutions, while serving as a fallback mechanism when the internal knowledge base contains gaps or outdated information.

From static models to dynamic agents

A critical advancement in TechSolve's architecture was the evolution from basic LLM implementations to sophisticated agent-based systems. This transformation fundamentally expanded the capabilities and autonomy of the AI solution in addressing complex enterprise needs.

LangChain transforms isolated language models into enterprise-grade agents that demonstrate sophisticated capabilities far beyond what direct API access would enable:

- **Distributed knowledge access**: Seamlessly retrieve and synthesize mission-critical information from multiple repositories, integrating structured database queries with unstructured document retrieval
- **Conversational persistence**: Maintain coherent memory across extended multi-turn interactions, preserving context without repetition and adapting to evolving user needs
- **Sequential reasoning**: Decompose complex problems into manageable sub-tasks, pursuing multi-step reasoning paths that are impossible through direct prompting alone
- **Tool utilization**: Dynamically invoke specialized capabilities, including calculators, code interpreters, and structured API calls, based on contextual requirements
- **Decision transparency**: Provide explicit reasoning traces documenting tool selection, information evaluation, and synthesis approaches for governance and auditability

This agent-based architecture fundamentally advances how AI systems operate within complex organizations. While traditional models excel at narrow prediction tasks, LangChain agents demonstrate emergent capabilities in knowledge synthesis, process automation, and multi-step reasoning across both structured and unstructured enterprise data. Beyond reasoning and prediction, these agents are also able to pursue defined goals by dynamically selecting tools, executing workflows, and coordinating actions to deliver end-to-end outcomes.

LangChain agent workflow

Agents are now a core part of modern AI implementations, since they enable systems to reason across multiple tools and data sources. However, the degree of agent involvement has a major impact on both performance and how deterministic the results are. To balance flexibility with reliability, many organizations add guardrails – constraints and validation checks that help keep responses consistent and aligned with business requirements.

Within TechSolve's system, the workflow follows six key stages that transform user queries into actionable insights.

User query input

Users submit natural language queries ranging from simple factual questions ("What's the compatibility matrix for version 4.2?") to complex technical inquiries ("Why might the inventory reconciliation module fail after a multi-currency transaction?"). Each query undergoes initial preprocessing, including the following:

- Entity extraction, identifying product components, versions, and technical concepts
- Intent classification, determining whether the query seeks factual information, procedural guidance, or problem diagnosis
- Disambiguation detection, identifying potential ambiguities requiring clarification

Intelligent routing

The agent applies sophisticated reasoning to determine the optimal processing route and tool sequence:

- For straightforward factual queries, it may trigger direct vector retrieval
- For complex troubleshooting scenarios, it may initiate a multi-step process combining retrieval, reasoning, and potentially web search
- For ambiguous queries, it may generate clarification sub-questions before proceeding

This dynamic routing creates a customized processing pipeline for each query, leveraging the LLM's reasoning capabilities to orchestrate a sequence of operations tailored to the specific information need.

Contextual augmentation

For knowledge-intensive queries, the agent queries the vector database to enrich the LLM prompt with relevant contextual data:

- Advanced techniques, such as hybrid retrieval, combine semantic similarity with keyword matching
- Metadata filtering restricts results based on recency, authority, and relevance criteria

- Multi-stage retrieval performs initial broad searches followed by focused refinement
- Reranking algorithms optimize the final selection of knowledge fragments

These techniques ensure optimal information selection from authoritative documentation, historical cases, and previous interactions, providing the LLM with precisely the context needed to generate accurate, helpful responses.

Web search (conditional)

When internal knowledge proves insufficient – particularly for recent updates or emerging issues – the agent performs targeted web searches:

- Automatically reformulates queries to optimize for search engine relevance
- Executes searches with strategic scope limitations (e.g., site-specific queries)
- Filters and validates results based on source credibility and content relevance
- Extracts and summarizes key information before integration into the response context

This conditional augmentation ensures the system remains current even as the underlying knowledge landscape evolves, bridging the gap between internal documentation and real-world developments.

Response generation

With comprehensive context assembled – potentially comprising internal knowledge, web search results, and conversation history – the agent feeds this information into the LLM for synthesis:

- Generates responses that directly address the user's query with appropriate detail and complexity
- Maintains consistent terminology aligned with organizational standards
- Provides explicit source attribution enabling verification when needed
- Formats information optimally based on content type (procedures as steps, compatibility as tables, etc.)

The result is a coherent response that integrates multiple knowledge sources while preserving the natural, helpful tone that makes LLMs particularly effective for knowledge transfer.

Feedback loop

A sophisticated feedback mechanism captures both explicit ratings and implicit signals:

- Users provide direct feedback through thumbs up/down ratings and optional comments
- Interaction metrics track which responses lead to follow-up questions versus resolution
- Usage patterns identify effective versus problematic response patterns
- Regular A/B testing compares alternative prompting strategies and retrieval approaches

This continuous learning cycle enables systematic refinement of retrieval strategies, prompting approaches, and tool selection logic. In practice, this happens through techniques such as **Reinforcement Learning with Human Feedback (RLHF)**, where user ratings are used to adjust model behavior, and context engineering, where prompts are iteratively refined based on previous successes and failures. Together, these methods create a cycle of improvement that steadily increases system value over time.

Technical infrastructure

The deployment of TechSolve's generative AI knowledge system required a robust, scalable technical infrastructure capable of handling enterprise workloads while maintaining performance, reliability, and security. This section describes the underlying compute and orchestration technologies that support the system's operations.

Cloud compute architecture

TechSolve implemented a hybrid cloud architecture that balances scalability with regulatory compliance:

- **Primary environment**: Azure cloud infrastructure leveraging managed Kubernetes services for core processing components
- **Secondary systems**: On-premises deployment for processing regulated healthcare client data with stringent data residency requirements
- **Development/testing**: Containerized environments enabling consistent development regardless of deployment target
- **Disaster recovery**: Cross-region replication with automated failover capabilities and 15-minute RPO guarantees

This strategic approach provides maximum flexibility while addressing various regulatory and performance requirements across TechSolve's diverse client base.

While this hybrid approach balances scalability and compliance, cost management is an important consideration. Running core workloads on managed cloud services can lead to higher operating expenses, especially when usage scales unpredictably. On the other hand, maintaining on-premises infrastructure for regulated data requires upfront investment in hardware, ongoing maintenance, and dedicated staff. To mitigate knowledge cutoff effects for pre-trained models, the system uses targeted web search with credibility filtering [7]. TechSolve adopts a cost optimization strategy that includes auto-scaling policies, reserved cloud instances for predictable workloads, and resource monitoring to identify underutilized compute. These measures help ensure that compliance and performance goals are met without uncontrolled cost growth.

End-to-end system architecture

To provide a comprehensive view of TechSolve's implementation, this section examines the complete system architecture, showing how individual components integrate into a cohesive whole. This end-to-end perspective illustrates the relationships between user-facing interfaces, application logic, and underlying data infrastructure that collectively deliver the knowledge management solution.

The complete system architecture follows a three-tier model, as shown in *Figure 7.2*. It separates concerns while ensuring seamless interaction between components:

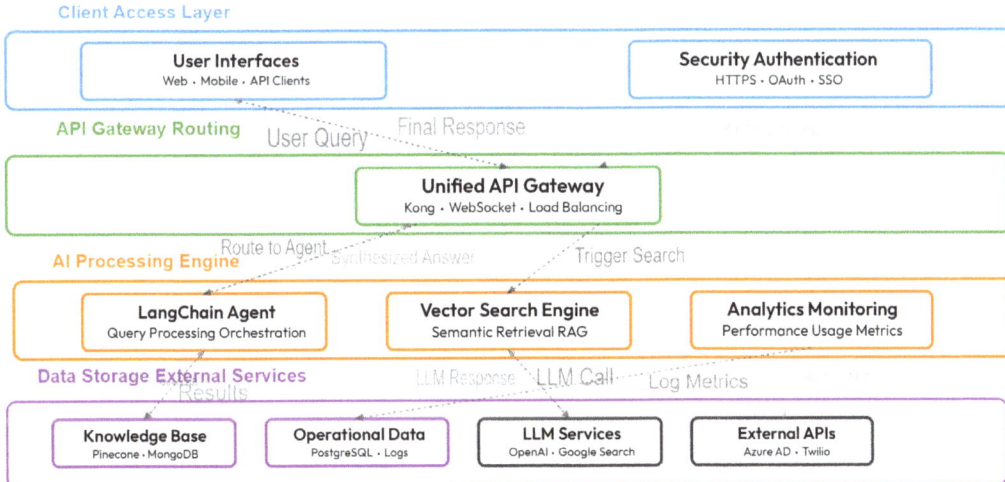

Figure 7.2: End-to-end system architecture: Web, mobile, and API access to AI-powered knowledge services

Client tier: User access and experience

At the top level, the client tier serves as the entry point for all user interactions:

- **Web interface:** Responsive design optimized for both desktop and tablet usage in technical support environments

- **Mobile application:** Native iOS and Android applications for field support scenarios

- **API access:** REST and GraphQL endpoints for integration with ticketing systems and custom tools

- **Security layer:** Comprehensive HTTPS implementation with certificate pinning and advanced authentication

Presentation tier: Interface orchestration

The middle layer houses the presentation tier, implemented as a Kubernetes cluster:

- **Orchestration web app:** React/Node.js application managing user interface state and interactions

- **API gateway:** Kong-based unified entry point providing request routing, rate limiting, and authentication

- **WebSocket service:** Real-time communication supporting streaming responses and typing indicators

- **Content Delivery Network (CDN) integration:** Global CDN, minimizing latency for static resources

Application tier: Business logic

The core processing occurs in the application tier:

- **Query processing service:** Manages request parsing, intent classification, and response generation

- **Vector database service:** Facilitates semantic search capabilities across knowledge repositories

- **Embedding service:** Transforms natural language into vector representations

- **Analytics service:** Provides insights through data aggregation and visualization

- **Workflow engine:** Orchestrates multi-step processes for complex support scenarios

Data tier: Information storage and retrieval

The foundation of the architecture is the data tier:

- **Vector database**: Pinecone implementation enabling efficient similarity searches
- **Document store**: MongoDB repositories managing unstructured content
- **Operational databases**: PostgreSQL systems handling transactional data
- **Logging/monitoring**: ELK stack capturing system performance metrics and user interactions

External services: Extending capabilities

The system integrates with specialized third-party solutions:

- **OpenAI API**: Provides advanced language understanding and generation capabilities
- **Google Search API**: Enables broader information retrieval beyond internal knowledge
- **Microsoft Entra ID**: Manages enterprise authentication and authorization
- **Twilio**: Enables SMS notifications for critical responses and updates
- **Elastic APM**: Provides application performance monitoring across the technology stack

User interaction patterns

While the technical architecture provides the foundation, the ultimate value of TechSolve's system is realized through its interactions with users. This section explores typical workflows and interaction patterns that demonstrate how support engineers and other stakeholders engage with the system to address customer needs efficiently.

To illustrate how different stakeholders interact with the system, TechSolve's architects documented key usage scenarios that capture common workflows.

Use case: Query resolution

This primary workflow represents the most common interaction pattern with TechSolve's knowledge system. When faced with a complex customer issue, support engineers leverage the AI system to rapidly access relevant information across organizational knowledge repositories, enabling faster and more accurate resolutions than previously possible through manual searches.

Primary actor: Support engineer

Secondary actor: AI system

Workflow:

1. The support engineer authenticates via SSO and navigates to the AI assistant interface.

2. They enter a detailed query describing the customer's technical problem.

3. The AI system processes the query through the LangChain agent, retrieving relevant knowledge chunks.

4. If needed, the system gathers supplementary data from Google web search for recent updates.

5. The LLM synthesizes a comprehensive response with explicit source citations.

6. The support engineer reviews the recommendation, potentially making modifications.

7. The final response is attached to the customer ticket, with all interactions logged for training.

Variations:

- If the system lacks sufficient information, it prompts for clarification or suggests knowledge gaps

- For sensitive customer data, the system uses on-premises processing paths with enhanced security

- When accessing restricted information, appropriate authorization checks prevent unauthorized disclosure

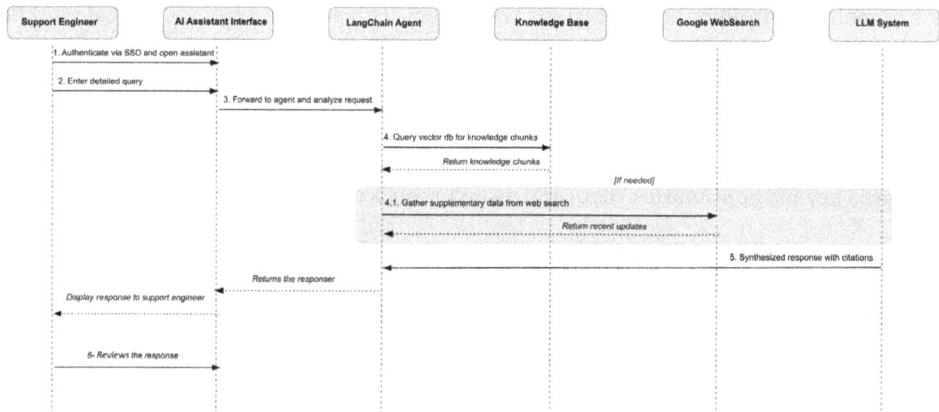

Figure 7.3: TechSolve's knowledge system sequence flow: end-to-end query processing pipeline

Business impact

The true measure of success for any technical implementation lies in its measurable business outcomes. This section analyzes the quantifiable results TechSolve achieved through their generative AI knowledge system, examining improvements across operational efficiency, customer experience, financial performance, and organizational culture.

To ensure these results were measured accurately, TechSolve established a comprehensive measurement framework. First, they captured a six-month baseline of pre-deployment data. **Operational metrics**, such as time to resolution, were extracted from their support ticketing system (Jira). **Customer experience data**, such as the **Net Promoter Score** (**NPS**) and satisfaction ratings, was collected via automated post-interaction surveys. **Financial data**, such as cost per ticket, was calculated by combining operational data with cost models from the finance department. Finally, data from the system's own **analytics service** was used to track usage patterns and knowledge contributions. All this information was aggregated into a central analytics dashboard for ongoing comparative analysis.

TechSolve's implementation of this architecture delivered transformative results across multiple dimensions:

Operational transformation

TechSolve's implementation produced dramatic improvements in support operations efficiency, transforming how engineers performed their daily work and significantly accelerating time to value for customers:

- **Resolution acceleration**: Average time to resolution decreased from 3 days to 4.7 hours (84% reduction)
- **Engineer productivity**: Time spent searching for information reduced from 60% to 26% of the workday
- **Capacity enhancement**: Support team accommodated 27% growth in ticket volume with only 8% staffing increase
- **Knowledge democratization**: Performance gap between senior and junior engineers reduced by 62%

Customer experience

Client satisfaction metrics showed substantial improvements as customers experienced faster, more consistent, and higher-quality support interactions:

- **Satisfaction metrics**: NPS increased by 37 points within 9 months of deployment
- **First contact resolution**: Rate improved from 34% to 71% through enhanced knowledge access
- **Consistent quality**: Variance in customer satisfaction ratings decreased by 58%
- **Response consistency**: Technical accuracy rate in responses increased from 82% to 97%

Financial outcomes

The business case for the implementation was validated through multiple financial metrics that demonstrated both cost savings and revenue growth:

- **Support economics**: Cost per ticket decreased by 31%, exceeding the original 25% target
- **Renewal impact**: Enterprise client renewal rates increased by 9% year over year
- **Expansion revenue**: Cross-sell and upsell revenue from existing clients grew by 14%
- **ROI achievement**: System achieved break-even on investment within 7.5 months of full deployment

Cultural evolution

Beyond measurable business outcomes, the system catalyzed significant organizational culture shifts that further amplified its impact:

- **Knowledge sharing**: Employee-contributed documentation increased by 143%
- **Collaboration enhancement**: Cross-functional knowledge exchange increased by 68%
- **Innovation acceleration**: Time to market for new features reduced by 22% through improved knowledge flow
- **Talent attraction**: Technical support job satisfaction scores increased by 41 points on internal surveys

Key architectural principles

Beyond the specific implementation details, TechSolve's experience yields valuable architectural principles applicable across diverse enterprise contexts. This section distills these core design patterns that contributed to the system's success, providing a framework that organizations can adapt to their own generative AI initiatives.

The TechSolve implementation embodies three fundamental design principles that can be applied across domains.

Retrieval-Augmented Generation (RAG)

RAG represents a paradigm shift in applied AI, combining the strengths of knowledge databases with generative capabilities:

- **Hallucination reduction**: Grounds outputs in verified sources, decreasing factual errors by 87%

- **Dynamic knowledge**: Enables information updates without model retraining, maintaining relevance as business environments evolve

- **Transparent sourcing**: Provides clear attribution for generated content, building trust and enabling verification

- **Efficiency optimization**: Reduces computational requirements by focusing model complexity on synthesis rather than memorization

This pattern has proven particularly valuable for enterprises with substantial proprietary knowledge, allowing them to leverage generative AI while maintaining accuracy and compliance.

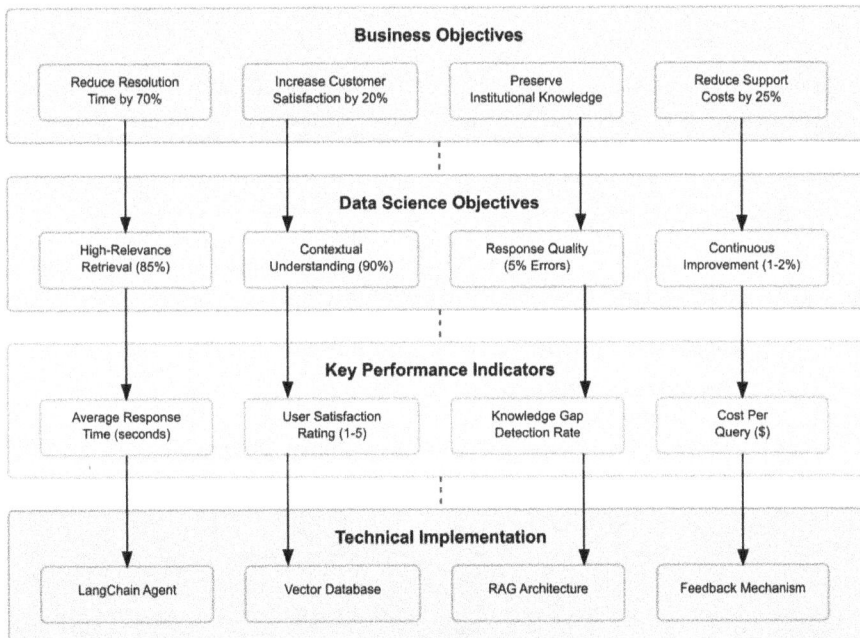

Figure 7.4: From business objectives to technical implementation: TechSolve's AI performance framework

Adaptive query routing

This architectural pattern implements intelligent workload distribution based on the following query characteristics:

- **Tiered processing**: Routes queries to appropriate resources based on complexity, from simple retrieval to sophisticated reasoning
- **Cost optimization**: Minimizes expenditure by matching computational resources to actual requirements
- **Response optimization**: Balances speed and thoroughness based on query urgency and importance
- **Fallback management**: Implements graceful degradation strategies when primary information sources prove insufficient

By matching processing approaches to query needs, this design principle maximizes both system efficiency and response quality across diverse usage scenarios.

Feedback-driven learning

The architecture implements systematic improvement through comprehensive feedback integration:

- **Multi-channel input**: Captures explicit ratings, implicit signals, and operational metrics to guide refinement
- **Controlled experimentation**: Utilizes A/B testing to evaluate alternative approaches for retrieval and generation
- **Performance monitoring**: Tracks key metrics, including accuracy, latency, and satisfaction across system components
- **Continuous adaptation**: Implements automated and manual refinement cycles that incrementally enhance capabilities

This learning ecosystem ensures the system becomes increasingly valuable over time, adapting to changing information needs and evolving language patterns.

Summary

This case study demonstrates how generative AI architecture for knowledge management can transform enterprise information systems. By integrating advanced LLMs with structured retrieval mechanisms, organizations can centralize scattered knowledge into unified, accessible frameworks [3][6][7].

TechSolve's implementation illustrates how thoughtfully designed AI architectures featuring layered components, robust data pipelines, and feedback-driven improvement mechanisms can improve support operations and enhance customer satisfaction [1].

The key insight: grounding AI responses in verified organizational knowledge through retrieval augmentation, maintaining clear data provenance, and establishing continuous feedback loops [3][5][2].

These architectural patterns extend beyond knowledge management to a wide range of enterprise applications, providing a blueprint for AI integration that balances innovation with governance and scalability with reliability [1].

As generative AI continues to mature, the architectural principles outlined here will remain essential guides for translating technological potential into sustainable business transformation [1][5].

References

1. Bass, Len, Paul Clements, and Rick Kazman. *Software Architecture in Practice: Software Architect Practice*. Addison-Wesley, 2012.

2. Lewis, Grace. "Getting Started with the NIST AI Risk Management Framework." SEI Blog, Carnegie Mellon University, 2023.

3. Gao, Jianfeng, et al. "Retrieval-Augmented Generation for Knowledge-Intensive NLP Tasks." *Advances in Neural Information Processing Systems*, 2020.

4. LangChain. "Agents." LangChain Documentation, 2023.

5. National Institute of Standards and Technology. "AI Risk Management Framework (AI RMF)." NIST, 2023.

6. Bommasani, Rishi, et al. "On the Opportunities and Risks of Foundation Models." arXiv preprint arXiv:2108.07258, 2021.

7. Zhao, Wayne Xin, et al. "A Survey of Large Language Models." arXiv preprint arXiv:2303.18223, 2023.

Unlock this book's exclusive benefits now

UNLOCK NOW

Scan this QR code or go to https://packtpub.com/unlock, then search this book by name.

Note: Keep your purchase invoice ready before you start.

8

Insights and Future Directions

We have made the case for how to build AI-enabled systems. Building AI-enabled systems is a challenge. There exist high expectations for the system and the likelihood that the software system is complex. There are several ways for a software development effort to fail; these range from not understanding key requirements, a technology not performing as expected, an erroneous system design, and compute, storage, or data flows being misunderstood. A major driver for failure is that humans can lose trust in the system if outputs are inconsistent, wrong, or just not sensible. AI-enabled systems have these risks plus algorithmic complexity, sensitive to off-nominal scenarios, and data inputs being off. A key driver of AI system failures is that users lose trust or have low confidence in the results provided by the system. AI-enabled systems must be built from inception so that they will utilize AI technologies. These systems must address decision-making without a human in the full inference or control cycle. The authors propose that architecture concepts and practices provide a mechanism to tame complexity and ensure that the correct system is built and built correctly.

Architecture

The role of an architect is both centuries old and a modern practice. This role cuts across many domains where complex systems are built. One now hears of architects in domains from semiconductors, aerospace, software, devices, autonomous systems, robotics, and others. The case has been made for the use of architecture concepts to deliver AI-enabled software systems. The implementation of disciplined architecture processes provides for a coherent vision of the end system. It also ensures that the correct system is being built. This is done by giving time and space for the key stakeholders, a mechanism to have their needs, desires, and concerns communicated. The architect team also has the charge of providing documentation. This documentation provides a mechanism to enable unity of effort across the technical team from requirements engineers, systems engineers, software engineers, and testers. Taking a holistic perspective, the architect ensures that a balanced design and appropriate mitigations are put in place.

If one takes away only one lesson from this book, it is that an architect must identify, communicate, document, and ensure that designs satisfy the non-functional requirements of the system. Almost certainly, the designs to meet the non-functional requirements of the end system impact the AI implementation, and vice versa.

The architect is pivotal for the execution of the engineering and building of the end system. The architect abstracts and usually conducts the system partitioning to enable the execution of software development across teams so that a unity of effort exists. The software engineering teams require documentation to understand how their respective parts of the system fit into the greater whole of the system. The documentation developed by the architect should encompass both written documents and modeling diagrams. The written artifacts should be, at a minimum, a concept of operations, a requirements specification, and key use cases. The modeling diagrams should include a logical block, activity, sequence, interface, use case, and state machine diagrams. Finally, there should be a diagram of the physical compute, storage, and networking hardware and specifications that are to be used. The architect must also work with the project and program managers to inform project control, scope, schedule, and resource management. The architect provides insight and feedback to inform project management tasks.

Building AI-enabled systems

We discussed the importance of software engineering for successful systems deployment. As of this writing, AI systems are primarily realized in software. Thus, one needs to grapple with classic software engineering risks. It was highlighted that the AI models or techniques used will most likely not be developed from the ground up. There exist many open source software libraries or references to lean on to build the major components of a system. In successfully built systems, a key enabler is to develop the system faster, for more time to develop, prototype, test, and learn.

The system and use of AI are very specific to the organization, domain, and needs of the stakeholders. It is naive to think that one can simply lift or update a prior system built for another domain.

It was pointed out that the overall complexity of systems drives software development risks. A disciplined approach and use of software building methodologies mitigate development risks. We highlighted the role of integration risks and methods to mitigate those risks. Integration efforts need to be accounted for and continuously considered.

Finally, the role of the architect in project management was highlighted. Many times, development teams and groups are organized around the software architecture itself.

The architect provides insight into how well a system is being built and whether key project milestones are occurring and at the expected level of cost and schedule. They also have a role in informing the staffing needs of the project.

Data engineering

A principal insight in this new era of data analytics and science is that a system's effectiveness is dependent on the quality of the data. This truism applies to the training and configuring of models, inference, the validation processes, and the production data. This has led to the emergence of a new engineering sub-specialty: the data engineer.

The data engineer must deal with the volume, velocity, variety, and provenance of the total data ecosystem. The field of data engineering is still in its early stages. These activities are now recognized as an engineering sub-specialty rather than "just data processing." When one engineers a system, the concepts and processes of architecture come to the fore. The data engineering efforts require the scoping of the data volumes, processing needs, storage capacity, and networking infrastructure. These analyses impact the planning of required hardware and software tooling.

As part of the architecting process, considerations must be made for the role of data quality. Data quality spans integrity, format, and consistency. We discussed how the architect needs to ensure that data quality concerns and issues are readily addressed either through active means or fallback capabilities. Of note is that data quality issues many times lead to errors or inconsistencies that can impact the trust of the inferences made by the system.

To reiterate, key components of the data engineering process require a first-order understanding of datasets themselves and the computing characteristics to enable the execution of models.

Data analytics and models

The heart of an AI system is the learning component – the place where the "smarts" of the system reside. Matching the right technique to customer objectives drives the technical teams' implementations. Many times, an architecture must be able to support different types of techniques to solve a specific problem: the importance of matching the relevant technique to a customer domain and the importance of visualization, and how the architecture should be used for capturing model performance metrics.

It is important to address model quality monitoring to aid in troubleshooting and monitoring of the system. The use of canaries and robust gold standard testing is key so that the decisions that are driven by the model are correct.

The authors are quite confident that many more techniques will be created and deployed. It is the charge of the architect to design and build robust systems to deal with this uncertainty. The aspiring AI architect should take this challenge head-on.

Conceptual design

As we have said throughout the book, the architect defines the conceptual foundations of the system to be built. The conceptual design captures the abstractions, functions, actors, and processes of the to-be-built system. The conceptual design and its associated artifacts should guide the reasoning, clarification, communication, and planning that underpin the actual system development. We highlighted that some of the key aspects of the conceptual design are to enable the communication of a clear rationale of the system and the value the new system shall deliver. The conceptual design documents the limitations of the current system. It also documents the challenges that need to be overcome and opportunities to be realized.

As has been laid out, the conceptual design activities should identify the major objectives of the system and how AI will be used. During this phase, the architect needs to balance the many stakeholders of the new system. A key consideration is the end user of the system and how the new system shall impact them. The conceptual design should also inform the non-technical aspects of the system development, such as cost and schedule constraints.

Known and true approaches to realize these are to use scenarios and conduct requirements engineering processes. These processes should be done at the very start of the project and revisited as systems development occurs. By revisiting requirements engineering processes, the impact of learning and feedback can be captured and inform further development. The development of scenarios and the conduct of requirements engineering must involve the full span of stakeholders to mitigate the risk that a key requirement is missed or misunderstood.

Not all systems development efforts are the same. Some projects may be as small as a few engineers to many dozens of engineers or more, but the value of documentation is constant, despite the size of the project. The documentation can span simple PowerPoint slides, spreadsheets, and full enterprise diagramming tools and requirements management databases. These documents should also be managed under a configuration control mechanism, as they can be a formal contract deliverable for the project.

The conceptual design culminates with a series of artifacts:

- **Concept of operations document**: This document describes the to-be-built system from the perspective of the user. It captures the key business goals and objectives that the system is to help realize. It lays out the major constraints and assumptions that underpin the system's development, and the metrics and attributes that are used to judge the performance and acceptance of the system.

- **Requirements specifications**: This document uses traditional requirements engineering processes of customer elicitation, workshops, brainstorming, modeling and simulation, mock-ups, and prototyping to describe all the many facets of what an operational system needs to do to ensure that it is successfully built.

- **Modeling diagrams**: The key diagrams here are use case diagrams, logical structure, behavioral diagrams, physical allocation, and interface definitions. This set of artifacts provides insight into the requirements specifications and aids in system design efforts. These diagrams also enable a first understanding of how the system is going to work.

- **Technical development plan**: This document details both the project capability that needs to be realized and the associated schedule gates.

Design, integration, and testing

A key theme we tried to convey was that an architect's role does not stop with the conceptual design. As an architect, one is judged by what is built and how well the system performs. A successful system is one that meets the many needs of the customer and that delivers the value expected of it. It is at this phase that the transition goes to actual development, and software engineering occurs. A critical role the architect plays is to ensure that the key non-functional or quality requirements are realized in the design.

We discussed the use of tactics and patterns to build software. In looking to solve existing design challenges, the use of tactics and patterns has shown itself to be quite powerful. The tactics and patterns we laid out are some that the authors found helpful. We think the use of tactics and patterns aids in managing complexity and improves communications across the engineering teams. The use of patterns is not a strict mandate. In building complex software, every system, use case, domain, and customer is different, so the use of tactics and patterns is left to the judgment of the architect.

Once the software is realized in code, the need for integration and testing comes to the fore. Integration should be done methodically and be timely. Many times, it is at integration that system-level effects are first realized. Integration challenges must be addressed from a holistic perspective. What one engineer would consider a minor change may have dramatic impacts on another part of the system. Integration is also where the potential friction comes out within and between teams. As mentioned, it is here that the big picture and vision of the architect can be used to ensure that integration remedies do not contradict or compromise the software system.

Finally, the architect at the end of development activities reviews test plans and testing results.

In modern software practices, there should be a culture of continuous testing. This ensures that errors and misunderstandings are discovered as soon as possible. The notion of waiting for a single point in time or event to do testing is a recipe for disaster. Testing should cover as many layers of the system, test interfaces, and load testing to ensure that the design and implementation are correct. The architect uniquely certifies that the correct system was built correctly.

Future directions of AI and architecture

AI systems and advanced software are going to continue to redefine many domains. There will be many new opportunities identified where AI technology can be used in a new or novel manner. The building of AI systems on a large scale and across our many areas of life is just beginning. Future directions for software development should look to aid in the requirements engineering of systems that involve decision-making for both inference and control. Robust modeling and simulation standards for the development of AI systems shall aid in specifying the overall quality and reliability of systems.

A future enabler for the design process includes the human as both a user and contributor to system functionality. Also, the use of tactics and patterns for AI systems needs to be better defined and given more specificity. Robust tactics need to be defined and capture how designs can be impacted by AI-centric patterns. We also need to address that software development itself is now being impacted by AI technologies. These new tools for development are powerful, can save time, and can give interesting insight, but they are not a replacement for the high cognitive thinking that is done by an architect.

Looking ahead, AI agents are poised to take on much more than simple automation. With the continued advancement of large language models and generative AI, these agents are becoming capable digital collaborators. They will be able to reason, learn from experience, and coordinate with other systems to achieve complex goals. In the near future, we can expect to see networks of agents working across industries, improving workflows, supporting decision-making, and enhancing human capabilities. This book is designed not only to help you build intelligent systems today but also to prepare you to take part in shaping the intelligent systems of the future.

Moving forward

The book has laid out a whirlwind of concepts, insights, and lessons learned. The best way to master this field is by doing – doing concepts of operations, working on defining use cases, conducting requirements elicitation, modeling, design activities, conducting testing, and working with customers. Learning how to be a competent architect is hard, and there are no guaranteed right guides or processes. We hope this book can be used as a reference for developing one's architectural knowledge and instincts. The journey to becoming an architect is like steadily climbing a never-ending mountain – but this just makes the view get better.

Good luck. Go forth and build systems that impact us all!

9

Unlock Your Book's Exclusive Benefits

Your copy of this book comes with the following exclusive benefits:

⊙ Next-gen Packt Reader
✦ AI assistant (beta)
▣ DRM-free PDF/ePub downloads

Use the following guide to unlock them if you haven't already. The process takes just a few minutes and needs to be done only once.

How to unlock these benefits in three easy steps

Step 1

Have your purchase invoice for this book ready, as you'll need it in *Step 3*. If you received a physical invoice, scan it on your phone and have it ready as either a PDF, JPG, or PNG.

For more help on finding your invoice, visit https://www.packtpub.com/unlock-benefits/help.

> **Note:** Did you buy this book directly from Packt? You don't need an invoice. After completing Step 2, you can jump straight to your exclusive content.

Step 2

Scan this QR code or go to `https://packtpub.com/unlock`.

On the page that opens (which will look similar to Figure X.1 if you're on desktop), search for this book by name. Make sure you select the correct edition.

| ‹packt› | Search... | | | | | | | Subscription | 🛒 0 | 👤 |

| Explore Products | Best Sellers | New Releases | Books | Videos | Audiobooks | Learning Hub | Newsletter Hub | Free Learning |

Discover and unlock your book's exclusive benefits

Bought a Packt book? Your purchase may come with free bonus benefits designed to maximise your learning. Discover and unlock them here

Discover Benefits — Sign Up/In — Upload Invoice

Need Help?

✦ **1. Discover your book's exclusive benefits** ^

🔍 Search by title or ISBN

CONTINUE TO STEP 2

👥 **2. Login or sign up for free** ∨

☁ **3. Upload your invoice and unlock** ∨

Figure X.1: Packt unlock landing page on desktop

Step 3

Once you've selected your book, sign in to your Packt account or create a new one for free. Once you're logged in, upload your invoice. It can be in PDF, PNG, or JPG format and must be no larger than 10 MB. Follow the rest of the instructions on the screen to complete the process.

Need help?

If you get stuck and need help, visit `https://www.packtpub.com/unlock-benefits/help` for a detailed FAQ on how to find your invoices and more. The following QR code will take you to the help page directly:

Note: If you are still facing issues, reach out to `customercare@packt.com`.

‹packt›

Other Books You May Enjoy

If you enjoyed this book, you may be interested in these other books by Packt:

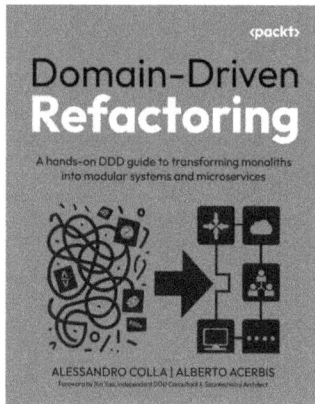

Domain-Driven Refactoring

Alessandro Colla, Alberto Acerbis

ISBN: 978-1-83588-910-7

- Find out how to recognize the boundaries of your system's components
- Apply strategic patterns such as bounded contexts and ubiquitous language
- Master tactical patterns for building aggregates and entities
- Discover principal refactoring patterns and learn how to implement them
- Identify pain points in a complex code base and address them
- Explore event-driven architectures for component decoupling
- Get skilled at writing tests that validate and maintain architectural integrity

Clean Architecture with Python

Sam Keen

ISBN: 978-1-83664-289-3

- Apply Clean Architecture principles idiomatically in Python
- Implement domain-driven design to isolate core business logic
- Apply SOLID principles in a Pythonic context to improve code quality
- Structure projects for maintainability and ease of modification
- Develop testing techniques for cleanly architected Python applications
- Refactor legacy Python code to adhere to Clean Architecture principles
- Design scalable APIs and web applications using Clean Architecture

Packt is searching for authors like you

If you're interested in becoming an author for Packt, please visit authors.packt.com and apply today. We have worked with thousands of developers and tech professionals, just like you, to help them share their insight with the global tech community. You can make a general application, apply for a specific hot topic that we are recruiting an author for, or submit your own idea.

Share your thoughts

Now you've finished *Architecting AI Software Systems*, we'd love to hear your thoughts! Scan the QR code below to go straight to the Amazon review page for this book and share your feedback or leave a review on the site that you purchased it from.

https://packt.link/r/1804615978

Your review is important to us and the tech community and will help us make sure we're delivering excellent quality content.

Index

V

W

www.ingramcontent.com/pod-product-compliance
Lightning Source LLC
Chambersburg PA
CBHW081104220326
41598CB00038B/7226